THE K
AMONG US

Why Jesus' ascension matters

The King is among us

Other books by Roy Lawrence

Christ With Us, SU, 1997
Finding Hope and Healing through the Bible, SPCK, 2000
How to Pray When Life Hurts, SU, 2003[2]
Invitation to Healing, Kingsway, 1979
Journey into Mystery, SPCK, 1999
Make Me a Channel, SU, 1996
The Practice of Christian Healing, SPCK, 1998

THE KING IS AMONG US

Why Jesus' ascension matters

Roy Lawrence

© Roy Lawrence 2004
First published 2004
ISBN 1 85999 771 6

Scripture Union, 207–209 Queensway,
Bletchley, MK2 2EB, England, UK
Email: info@scriptureunion.org.uk
Website: www.scriptureunion.org.uk

Scripture Union Australia
Locked Bag 2, Central Coast Business Centre, NSW 2252
Website: www.su.org.au

Scripture Union USA
P.O. Box 987, Valley Forge, PA 19482
Website: www.scriptureunion.org

Scripture quotations, unless otherwise attributed, are taken from the Holy Bible, New International Version. Copyright © 1973, 1978, 1984 by International Bible Society. Anglicisation copyright © 1979, 1984, 1989. Used by permission of Hodder and Stoughton Ltd.

British Library Cataloguing-in-Publication Data.

A catalogue record for this book is available from the British Library.

Cover design by ie design

Printed and bound by Creative Print and Design (Wales), Ebbw Vale

℘ Scripture Union is an international Christian charity working with churches in more than 130 countries, providing resources to bring the good news about Jesus Christ to children, young people and families and to encourage them to develop spiritually through the Bible and prayer.

As well as our network of volunteers, staff and associates who run holidays, church-based events and school Christian groups, we produce a wide range of publications and support those who use our resources through training programmes.

To Andrew Clark
and all his colleagues at Scripture Union
who are working so hard
and so imaginatively
to bring our nation back to the Bible

Contents

The stories in this book are all based on real events, but in order to preserve anonymity, most of the names and some of the details have been changed.

Chapter 1
The forgotten festival

The bathroom scales in our home have a strange habit. Sometimes they flick past one weight or another without registering it at all. The red figures on the little electronic display panel can jump from – say – 69.5 kilos straight to 70.5 kilos as though there were no such weight as 70 kilos in between.

Every time this happens it reminds me of the way many of our churches behave in Britain today. As we seek to teach the faith, we have often picked up the habit of bypassing a number of quite fundamental Christian truths. We behave as though they had no place in the Bible or the creeds or in our historic doctrines. One of the instances of this is that in my own church, the Church of England, we have increasingly developed the custom of leapfrogging from the season of Easter to Whit Sunday, virtually ignoring the season of Ascension, which ought to come in between.

This used not to be so. When I was a boy, attending our local C of E school, every Ascension Day all the pupils were taken into the parish church for a service, and afterwards the rest of the day was a holiday. So we were well pleased when the festival of the ascension came along.

I suppose that in those days the school was guided by the old Prayer Book, where Ascension Day was accorded great prominence. Not only did it have its own Collect, Epistle and Gospel but it had its own Proper Preface in the Communion Service too, which put it on a level with Christmas, Easter, Whit Sunday and Trinity Sunday. This Prayer Book perspective stands in line with the tradition of the early Christian church. Augustine tells us that in his time Ascension Day was universally cherished and celebrated by Christians. This observance led him to suppose that it was a festival that might well have been instituted by the apostles themselves. He goes as far as to say: 'This is that festival which confirms the grace of all the festivals together, without which the profitableness of every festival would have perished.'[1] His enthusiasm for the ascension was later shared by many of the Reformers. John Calvin wrote: 'The Ascension of Christ ... is one of the chief points of our faith.'[2]

By contrast, if you were to go out now on to the streets of Britain with a vox-pop microphone on Ascension Day and ask passers-by what day it was, you would be met by totally blank stares. 'It's just an ordinary Thursday,' people would say. Even serious regular churchgoers could not be guaranteed to do much better. I know from years of frustrating experience as vicar in a succession of North of England parishes how difficult it has been to coax people into church on Ascension Day. In my last parish it should have been easier, because Ascension Day was a sort of foundation festival, the day on which the church's memorial stone had been laid and also the day on which we used to hold our annual Confirmation Service. Yet still there were many who seemed largely unaware of the nature and purpose of the festival.

Perhaps there are two main reasons why Ascension Day is so easily forgotten these days.

The first is that people find it difficult to picture just what happened on the Mount of Ascension. Most of us can create a mental picture of the baby Jesus lying in a manger in a stable on the first Christmas Day. We can also picture him tramping the dusty roads of Palestine with his disciples during his three years of itinerant ministry. We can probably picture him hanging on the cross, horrendously put to death by a Roman execution squad, and mysteriously bearing our sins as he died. We can perhaps picture the discovery of the empty tomb on Easter Day. Maybe we can even have some sort of a stab at imagining our Lord's resurrection body, during the forty days of Easter, when he appeared again and again to astonished groups of his followers. But we find it very hard to produce a credible mental picture in which Jesus ascends from a mountaintop towards heaven rather like a slow-motion space-rocket. The attempt is not made any easier by the fact that probably most of us no longer think of heaven as 'up there' or even 'out there'.

The second reason is perhaps even more fundamental. Not only do we find it hard to imagine what happened on the Mount of Ascension; we also find it difficult to fathom the meaning and purpose of it. Few people seem to have much idea what the ascension actually achieved and how it can influence our lives today.

This book is a quest for lost truth. It is the result of a treasure hunt that has occupied me for several years. I suppose it started as a theological exercise, motivated by a sense of intrigue and curiosity, but I soon found that discovering the treasure of the ascension changed my life. I believe it can do the same for others. If the Christian church can once again come to understand the message of the mysterious events that took place on the Mount of Ascension, we shall find that the result involves much more than brushing the dust off an old, neglected doctrine.

Augustine was right. When the ascension of Jesus comes to life for us, everything else in the Christian faith will also acquire a new and vital significance. There will be new point and purpose and what Augustine calls 'profit'[3] in all the Christian festivals and a new power in our personal Christianity. But don't take my word for it – or Augustine's, for that matter. Find out for yourself. Come with me on the treasure hunt.

Chapter 2
What happened on the mountain?

The first stage of the treasure hunt must be to attempt a reconstruction of the course of events that led up to and culminated in the mysterious experiences of Ascension Day.

Can you imagine yourself with the disciples on the Mount of Ascension? It is not necessary to have been to the Holy Land in order to do so. Select any hill of your choice, perhaps from your own locality or one that has remained in your memory after a holiday. Let this be your mental setting for the ascension. If you have strong powers of imagination, you may actually be able to identify yourself with one of the disciples. Or it may be easier to be there as yourself, observing and participating in all that happens in your own right. This is a totally proper thing to do, for reasons we shall think about later.

As, in your imagination, you and the disciples stand on the mountain, you may all find your minds going back over the three years of Jesus Christ's travelling ministry, which have just come to an end. So much of it took place on one mountainside or another. Mountains had already had a major part in the development of the history of the Israelite people. It was on a mountain that Moses received the Ten

Commandments (Exod 19:17 – 20:17). It was on a mountain
that Elijah defeated the prophets of Baal (1 Kings 18:20–40).
The Psalms and the Prophets are full of references to mountains, as any biblical concordance will show. In just the same
way, mountains were important in the life and work of
Jesus. There was the Mount of Temptation at the outset of his
ministry. The disciples were not present at the time, but he
subsequently told his followers about his experiences in the
craggy, deserted place where he found himself waging spiritual warfare as he wrestled with Satanic pressure to mis-
direct the course of his future life (Matt 4:8). And there were
further places of hillside solitude, which were spiritually
important for Jesus, because he used them as retreats for
prayer (Luke 6:12).

On these occasions the disciples could only watch him
come and go. But they were all present on the Mount of
Ordination, when he appointed them to be his apostles
(Mark 3:13). They were present too on the mountain that
became an open-air pulpit for his most famous sermon
(Matt 5:1,2), and on the hillside where he fed 5,000 hungry
people (John 6:3). And they could certainly never forget the
Mountain of Healing, on which Jesus brought new wholeness of body, mind and spirit to crowds of sick and disabled
people (Matt 15:29–31). Then, too, a privileged few were
allowed access to the amazing Mount of Transfiguration,
where time and eternity fused together as, before their
astonished gaze, 'His face shone like the sun, and his clothes
became as white as the light' (Matt 17:2). And what about
the mountain that, Jesus claimed, not only he but his followers could actually move by the power of faith (Matt
17:20)? You may like to read these texts again and allow the
events they describe to run through your mind – as they
would certainly have run through those of the disciples on

the Mount of Ascension.

Then, more recently, there was the terrible place where Jesus had been crucified. Many of us find ourselves thinking of it as, in the words of Mrs C F Alexander's hymn, 'the green hill far away, / Without a city wall'. But that description is unlikely to be historically accurate. The name of the place in Hebrew was *Golgotha*. In Latin it was *Calvaria*. In Greek it was *Kranion*. They all mean 'Skull'. So rather than a 'green hill', we should probably think in terms of a barren, skull-shaped knoll. In any event, whatever its appearance may have been, 'Skull Hill' could not have been far from the minds of the disciples as they subsequently stood on the Mount of Ascension. They would not at that stage have had a considered theology of atonement in their minds. Later Mrs Alexander was to write:

He died that we might be forgiven,
He died to make us good,
That we might go at last to heaven,
Saved by his precious blood.

But at the ascension this sort of theological understanding was not available to the apostles. If you are to feel one with them at this time, you will have to imagine the doubts and confusion that many of them were still experiencing (Matt 28:17). Love incarnate had been lynched on a cross. The religious hierarchy of the day had plotted it. A Roman death squad had executed it with brutal efficiency. And a baying, bloodthirsty mob had slavered over every moment. Behind it all were the sins of the human race as a whole, including your sins and mine.

The events had all been predicted many years before.

He was despised and rejected by men,
a man of sorrows, and familiar with suffering.
Like one from whom men hide their faces
he was despised, and we esteemed him not.

Surely he took up our infirmities
and carried our sorrows,
yet we considered him stricken by God,
smitten by him, and afflicted.
But he was pierced for our transgressions,
he was crushed for our iniquities;
the punishment that brought us peace was upon him,
and by his wounds we are healed.

Isaiah 53:3–5

Maybe these very words were echoing in the minds of the disciples on Ascension Day as they relived the anguish of the crucifixion.

Forty days, however, had now elapsed since the execution of Jesus – and what amazing days they had been! The obscenity of the crucifixion had been followed by the apparent impossibility of the resurrection. The bewildered apostles could hardly take it in. Not only had they seen the risen Christ themselves but, just in case they were tempted to think that their eyes were deceiving them, there were reports of sightings of Jesus by many other people too, sometimes individuals, sometimes small groups, sometimes large groups, and once a crowd of over five hundred people (1 Cor 15:3–8). And the sightings were not of someone who could just about drag himself from place to place, looking half-dead because he had been brutalised, tortured and drained of life; this risen Christ was full of light and life and power. It seemed that, though Love could be put to death, it could not be 'held' by death. Hate, though it kills, has death at its heart and will ultimately self-destruct, whereas Love, though it dies, has life at its heart and will rise again.

The disciples' minds must have been awash with conflicting emotions – joy and relief on the one hand and blank, confused incredulity on the other, a strange amalgam of simultaneous faith and doubt. See if you can identify with their feelings as, in their disorientated condition, they received their Lord's command to meet with him once more on what was to be the Mount of Ascension. For all their turmoil, they were not disobedient. And so it was that they found themselves on the mountain, as in your imagination you do too.

Picture yourselves waiting together, your minds full of memories of the life, death and resurrection of Jesus – and then suddenly he himself is in your midst! It is rather like a re-run of the events on the Mount of Transfiguration. His shining presence makes an immediate difference to you all. Your doubts are dwarfed by his deity. You are moved to worship (Matt 28:17).

And now he is speaking to you about himself and about all of you – words of revelation, of commission and of deep, abiding promise. You could all have listened to him for hours, but all too quickly he is gone. In the traditional phrase, 'a cloud hid him from sight' (Acts 1:9).

In my personal reconstruction of events I see the mist swirling about him as he speaks. It becomes so thick that he can no longer be seen. When it finally clears, Jesus is no longer there. I have seen something similar happen on a hillside in Yorkshire. In fact, it once happened while I was leading a course that dealt with the ascension at the

Bradford Diocesan Retreat House, Parceval Hall, near the
village of Appletreewick. As I spoke, through the picture
windows of the conference room we all watched the mist fall
and rise again on the surrounding hills. It was just as if God
was providing his own visual aid.

In Scripture the language used is that of ascent (Acts 1:9),
because this is a natural way to speak about achievement
and completion. We are not required to interpret it literally.
If we say that some young executives are high flyers, we are
not implying that they sprout wings and flap around the
ceiling of the board room. If we say they are rising to the top
of their firm, we are not suggesting that they will be given
offices in Portacabins on the roof of the company headquar-
ters. The same use was made of the metaphorical language
of ascent in the ancient world. This was particularly true in
a spiritual context. Thus the phrase 'go up' was used of visiting a temple, even if the temple was at sea level.

We need not, therefore, think of Jesus as having gone
either 'up there' or 'out there' in any literal sense after the
ascension.

So then, where is he in these post-ascension days? It is a
question we should not evade. For myself, I like to think of
him as now being in what I term a 'larger place', though even
as I write the words I am conscious of their inadequacy,
because he is no longer bound by time constraints or space
limitations. For him the ascension was a de-restriction, a lib-
eration, a re-entry into multi-dimensionalism, a reunion with
the infinite. Miraculously, at the incarnation he had become
small in order to reach out to small beings like ourselves. But
the message of the ascension is that he is small no longer.

Maybe I owe this thought to C S Lewis. In his science-
fiction-type fable *The Great Divorce*[1] he tells the story of a day
trip from hell to heaven. A group of citizens from hell seek

to alleviate the tedium of their lives by getting on a coach that then appears to rise, leaving the rain, the fog and the misery of hell far below, and scale the cliffs of heaven before allowing its motley assortment of passengers to alight and have the opportunity to do a spot of celestial sightseeing. For all the glories of heaven, they have no desire to stay. They actually prefer the selfishness and small-mindedness of hell to heaven's opportunities for love and growth.

The contrast between the smallness of hell and the largeness of heaven is one of the book's major themes. It means that, as far as the coach trip is concerned, although the bus seemed to scale many cliffs, it needed not so much to ascend as to 'expand'. Lewis' mentor George MacDonald explains to him: 'The voyage was not mere locomotion. The bus and all you inside were increasing in "size".'[2] When Lewis asks MacDonald to show him where they have come from, they have to go down on their hands and knees to look for the coach's starting-point. In order to search for hell they have to peer into a tiny crack in the soil of heaven, so small that a blade of heaven's grass can hardly be inserted into it. For heaven is infinite, whereas hell is infinitesimal. Or to put it another way, heaven is real, whereas hell is phantasmal. And according to Lewis, while you and I are on earth, we are in a state of flux somewhere between the two with a lot of thinking to do and a lot of choices to make, all concerned with growing or shrinking into one of our two possible destinies. He makes it clear his fable is no more than speculation, originating in his own mind, though with a bit of help from an American sci-fi magazine. But personally I find it helpful.

Reverting to the context of the ascension, Lewis has helped me to see that, though God the Son miraculously limited and restricted himself to such an extent at the incarnation that he put himself in our hands and within our history, a man among men and women, it had to be that at some point the perspective of eternity would reassert itself. This is what happened on the Mount of Ascension.

For the Son of God the years of deprivation and curtailment were now over – and yet part of the wonder of the ascension is that the incarnation has not been reversed. *He is still human,* and, just as he came into this world for us, lived and died for us and rose from the dead for us, so his ascension is *for us.*

Mighty Lord, in thine ascension,
We by faith behold our own.

Bishop Christopher Wordsworth

What, then, happened on the Mount of Ascension? It was the occasion on which the followers of Jesus were privileged to watch as he re-entered his true and eternal state of being. But he made it clear to them that he did so after accomplishing his mission. From the ascension onwards nothing would ever be the same for him or for us.

This brings us to the larger question, to which we shall be addressing ourselves from this point on. However we picture the sequence of events on the Mount of Ascension, what is the meaning of it all for us? What is the difference that it is designed to make to you and me?

Chapter 3
More than Independence Day

'It is for your good that I am going away,' said Jesus to his disciples (John 16:7). Soon after I was ordained, I took those words as a text for a sermon, because my post-ordination tutor had asked me to preach on the subject of the ascension. I used the old Authorised Version, as we did in those days – 'It is expedient for you that I go away' – and the sermon that resulted is still clear in my mind.

It started by telling the story of an occasion in my childhood, when, as a little boy, my father taught me to ride a bicycle. I sat somewhat precariously on the bicycle and pedalled, while Dad puffed up and down the road with me, keeping the machine steady. But one day, during the course of a lesson, I looked back to make some comment or other – only to find that to my horror Dad had let go and was standing fifty metres or so behind on the road. I was under my own steam, independent. In consequence, I promptly fell off. But unless my father had been willing to let go, I would never have learned to ride properly.

Something similar happened to the early church – so my sermon said – on the first Ascension Day. I reckoned that another name for the festival that commemorates it could be

'Independence Day', because there was a real sense in which Ascension Day was the occasion when Jesus 'let go'. Until then he had held his followers on course and they had been well content to have it so. While the bodily form of Jesus was with the church, both before and after the resurrection, the tendency of the early Christians was to cluster round him, to lean upon him, to depend upon him. If they were to become independent it was necessary that he should leave.

I saw a paradox in this, a contrast between human power and divine power. The tendency of human power, founded as it is on the fear of being weak, is to try to mould and influence those around it. Human power wants to master people, it wants to lessen their independence and individuality. But divine power, founded on absolute strength, works in quite the opposite way. Divine power tries to set free those it has created, to make them independent, to make them truly themselves. There is, of course, the danger that they will spoil themselves, just as there was the danger that I would fall off my bike when Dad let go. When applied to God's creation, this risk is a terrible thing. Human history is tainted with brutal wars and with every form of injustice. Human beings have degraded, bullied, hurt and destroyed one another, and have treated the rest of creation equally badly. This is the direct consequence of the risk involved in God's gift of freedom to us. God does not view this risk lightly. His Son's willingness to come among us and endure crucifixion for us is the measure of his concern. But for all that, God has not shown himself willing to take away human freedom, human independence. God has not shown himself willing to make us robots. 'It is expedient for you that I go away.'

There are various implications of this interpretation of the ascension with its stress on the importance of every individual's freedom and independence. For instance, it tells us something about the sort of relationships we ought to have with each other. In the world as we know it life can so easily degenerate into a power game. There is no shortage of control freaks, people trying to turn their spouses and partners into echoes of themselves, parents trying to manipulate their children, business executives bullying those who work under them, political and religious leaders brainwashing their followers, dictators brutalising their subjects. It is all quite sensible if our aim is what the world sees as power. But it was not the way of the Lord, who said, 'It is expedient that I go away', and it should not be the way of his followers. As Christians we are called to encourage those around us to become their truest and best selves, to grow to their own full stature as individuals. And in doing so we should, almost inadvertently, be growing to our own full stature ourselves.

There is an implication too as we consider some of the factors that make Christianity distinctive from other world religions. If we were Hindus or Buddhists, we should not set much store by the concept of individuality. We should consider personal individuality as, on the whole, a nuisance and an evil. We should see salvation in terms of absorption into God, of losing our identity in God, much as a raindrop loses its identity in the sea. This is not the Christian picture. Think of our Lord. After his death he did not jettison his humanity and merge into his Father. He ascended into heaven, humanity and all, and, just as he was, God-human, he sat and sits at the right hand of the Father, a person within the Godhead.

In an exalted way this provides the pattern for us. God does not call us to absorption. He calls us to be our own best selves with him and in him for all eternity. There is something of infinity in human nature. God calls us to discover it and enjoy it for ever. So the Christian doctrine of humanity, whether we view it in a temporal or an eternal context, is a very high one.

In my sermon, having looked at some of these implications, I concluded by saying that in the life of Christ, God had paid humankind four great compliments. He has considered human nature good enough to share at the incarnation, good enough to bear at the crucifixion, good enough to raise at the resurrection, and finally good enough to leave free and independent at the first Ascension Day. I remember that these words had quite a ring to them when I spoke them from the pulpit in St George's, Stockport, many years ago. When I sent the sermon off to my post-ordination tutor I was delighted to be awarded an alpha for it. But I have to admit that, on reflection, I do not think it was actually worth an alpha. It was true so far as it went, but I now reckon that it did not go all that far.

It is, of course, true that at a practical level we need to achieve some measure of independence if we are to succeed in life. Riding a bicycle provides just one illustration, but there are many more. When, as tiny toddlers, we are learning to walk, we have at some stage to let go of Mummy's hand. And how about learning to swim or to drive a car or to fly a plane? The moment of independence is crucial. The water-wings and the L-plates have to come off, and I well remember how a friend who is now a pilot grew in stature and confidence when he successfully completed his first solo flight. Students have to leave college. Trainees and apprentices have to branch out for themselves. That is the way life goes.

None of this, however, serves as an adequate parallel to what happened at the ascension of Jesus. It was much more than a passing-out parade for the disciples. Though it is true that the disciples were required to exercise a new degree of independence from that point on, my sermon was an over-simplification, and I have no doubt that the disciples would have seen many flaw-lines in it. For a start, they would not have regarded their new independence as a 'compliment'. It was a strange and unsought gift, and in some ways a terrible one. They would not have been able to bear it had it not been for the fact that with the gift and its challenges came unexpected and mysterious resources.

One of them was a new, deeply personal relationship with Jesus. Unaccountably, the one who said, 'It is expedient for you that I go away', was now more closely with them than ever. Paul never ceases to marvel at this. For him the heart of Christian living lies in the experience of being 'in Christ' (Greek, *en Christo*). I like the translation of these words in the Good News Bible as 'union with Christ'. Paul is said to use these words or their equivalent 164 times. We shall see later in this book that this union with Christ would not have been possible without the ascension. If Ascension Day is Independence Day, therefore, it celebrates not independence 'from' the Lord but 'in' the Lord.

Also, did you notice that my old sermon dealt with only half a text? It omitted the second and more important half of John 16:7: 'It is expedient for you that I go away' is not complete as a statement until it is followed by 'for if I go not away, the Comforter will not come unto you; but if I depart, I will send him unto you' (Authorised Version). The ascension was a bridge to Pentecost. It made possible the gift of the Holy Spirit as the living heart of the newly created Christian church. I shall be suggesting in a subsequent chapter that we make a serious mistake in our own lives if we try to take a shortcut to Pentecost without first going with the disciples to the Mount of Ascension.

Moreover, even the full version of the words recorded in

John 16:7 is only a tiny part of Christ's teaching at the time of his Ascension, much of it given on the Mount of Ascension itself. For instance, it is to that mountain that we must go if we would learn of Christ's para-cosmic kingship and of our own lives as subjects and ambassadors of the King. Moreover, it was on the Mount of Ascension that the disciples received a promise of the final return of Jesus at the end of the age. It was then that they learned of him as the one who would bring human history to its climax and consummation. They never forgot it – even though today's church often seems to do so. There were also practical lessons to be learned on that mountain about the nature of prayer and the basis of Christian healing and the empowerment of Christian living. Finally, the Mount of Ascension was in a real sense a gateway to eternity, a window into heaven. The disciples were perhaps closer at that moment than at any other to transcending time and glimpsing the life that is stronger than death, to which Jesus was returning and to which he calls each one of us, if we will open our eyes, our ears and our hearts to him.

We shall seek to draw closer to these mysteries as this book continues, but for the present perhaps we may return to the concept with which this chapter began. For behind it there lies a much larger truth. Although we should not have come into being without God's originating creativity, and although our continuation depends upon God's sustaining creativity, it does seem to be his will that we achieve a degree of independence that should logically be impossible. The Christian church should never be like a Communist or Fascist regime, which ruthlessly suppresses those who dare to think for themselves. It should not even be like a liberal nanny-state, which seeks to impose what it deems to be the best upon its citizens, whether they want it or not.

It is the teaching of the Bible that we are made in the image of God (Gen 1:26), and so each one of us is precious and unique. We have marred that image and have become less than ourselves in the process. We have deluded ourselves that self-centredness would bring us independence. But the opposite has proved to be the case. We are constantly in danger of becoming slaves, and our slavery can take many forms. We can be slaves to nothing more sinister than the fads and fashions of society. More seriously, we can be slaves to our own urge for wealth or power, or to an addiction – perhaps drugs, alcohol or nicotine – or to prejudice, or to a besetting sin that has us totally in its power. Self-centred humankind is far from free. But it is God's will that these and other forms of slavery should lose their control over us, so that each of us should have the opportunity to become his or her true self. God wants us to 'become mature people, reaching to the very height of Christ's full stature' (Eph 4:13, Good News Bible). That is the nature of the 'independence' that is God's plan and purpose for us. In order for that purpose to be achieved a miracle of generosity and love was needed, and we turn now to consider just how the ascension of Jesus became a necessary part of God's gospel plan to set us free.

Chapter 4
A festival of kingship

There can be no better teacher than Jesus himself, if we wish to deepen our understanding of any element within the Christian faith. So we are very fortunate to be able to access three important strands of his teaching about the ascension in the verses that conclude Matthew's Gospel. They are among the last words spoken on earth by Jesus, and are full of insight about the meaning of the ascension even though (unlike Luke and Mark) Matthew does not go on to describe the event itself.

The first of these strands lays claim to an authority and influence that cannot be confined by time or space, a kingship that extends well beyond this world. Jesus says, 'All authority in heaven and on earth has been given to me' (Matt 28:18).

Paul offers a remarkable meditation upon these words in his letter to the Philippians (2:6–11). It is usually thought to be based on a hymn current in the early church. The hymn was not necessarily written by Paul – it contains words he does not use elsewhere – but whether he wrote it or not, it seems to represent a fundamental strain of teaching among the first Christians.

It begins by pondering the enigma of the servanthood of Jesus. Jesus is described as 'in very nature God', and yet the hymn tells us that both by his life and by his death he accepted the role of a servant. This was in line with his own teaching that true greatness is to be measured not in earthly grandeur and power but in terms of our capacity for service (Matt 20:26,27). Here, as always, Jesus embodied his own teaching. So the hymn celebrates the servanthood he revealed in his life and death.

Yet the hymn also celebrates the fact that if the gospel is true the moment had to come when, for all the humility of his servant role, Jesus would be revealed in the greatness and glory that were intrinsically his. The ascension was pre-eminently that moment, because it was on the Mount of Ascension that

… God exalted him to the highest place
 and gave him the name that is above every name,
 that at the name of Jesus every knee should bow,
 in heaven and on earth and under the earth,
 and every tongue confess that Jesus Christ is Lord,
 to the glory of God the Father.

Philippians 2:9–11

It is the message of the ascension that Christ's authority and kingship will always be supreme and that his rule is the ultimate reality both in and beyond this world, no matter how completely human beings may choose to close their eyes and ears and hearts to this truth.

The Nicene Creed makes this point very graphically. It invites us to picture the ascended Christ as sitting 'on the right hand of the Father.' According to Luther the Father's right hand is the symbol of his omnipotence. The ascended Christ is one with that omnipotence and so 'his kingdom shall have no end'. The picture of Jesus 'sitting' rather than standing in this place of kingship and omnipotence is a sign of the completion of his mission and the permanence of his achievement. It is also a sign of his enthronement in glory. The Father has 'seated him at his right hand in the heavenly realms, far above all rule and authority, power and dominion, and every title that can be given, not only in the present age but also in the one to come' (Eph 1:20,21).

Ascension Day, then, is a festival of kingship. There are many references in the Bible to Christ the ascended King, sitting at the Father's right hand (eg Ps 110:1; Matt 26:64; Col 3:1; Heb 8:1; 1 Pet 3:22). The world, however, does not see Jesus in this magisterial way. This was made very clear in the early days of the Christian church. The Christian faith and its founder were the targets of insults at every level of society, ranging from the sneers that circulated in the emperor's court to the graffiti that could be found, then as now, in public places. One of these graffiti that has always lodged in my mind contained a crude picture of an early Christian standing before Jesus on the cross. Underneath is written: 'Alexamenos worships his God.' What makes the picture contemptuous is that the figure on the cross has a donkey's head! For only a donkey, it was thought, could possibly claim to be such a god.

There is similar scorn for Jesus and his followers in many parts of the world today. In much of the world Christians are actively derided and persecuted. More were martyred for their Christian faith in the twentieth century than in all the nineteen centuries beforehand put together. This persecution continues today. There is sometimes a curious conspiracy of silence in the popular press about this, but details can be found in magazines and prayer leaflets published by organisations such as Christian Solidarity Worldwide,[2] , Release International[3] and Jubilee Action.[4] Even though there is no such persecution in the UK, Christians can sometimes experience a degree of patronising scorn. For instance, on TV, people who go to church are again and again represented as wimps, weeds and bigots. This means that those who intend to take the Ascensiontide concept of the kingship of Christ seriously must be prepared to make a radical adjustment to the mindset we shall otherwise inherit from society.

Becoming a subject of Christ the King is no mere matter of academic theology. It involves a major upheaval in the way we live day by day, and we never know when a fundamental, life-changing decision may be called for through obedience to the laws of his kingdom.

I think, for example, of Stanley, who felt he had to leave the firm in which he occupied an executive position, because his company was turning a blind eye to a practice totally incompatible with his principles as a Christian. He knew he had to choose between his firm and his faith, and eventually, after a period of agonising soul-searching, he handed in his resignation. Ultimately, he obtained an even better position with another company, but not before undergoing a period of unemployment and ill health. It is not easy to serve Christ the King in a society that rejects that kingship.

Or there is Jonathan, who used to work in a cigarette factory but, after accepting the kingship of Christ, felt bound to change his job in view of the carcinogenic properties of nicotine. He has now been ordained and is exercising a very effective ministry.

There can also be a revolution in terms of personal life after becoming a subject of Christ the King. When Colin became a

Christian, he was in the course of having an affair with a married woman. They had been considering breaking up both his home and hers, but he could not help but realise that none of this was compatible with the rule of Jesus. It was Christ the King who brought him back to his wife and children. And I shall never forget Patrick, whose personal problem was an addiction to pornography but who knew when he became a committed Christian that his collection of porno magazines had to go. It was my privilege to help both Colin and Patrick get through these difficult times. One of my abiding memories of both was how much happier they both looked when they finally took the step of putting Jesus first. The laws of the kingdom of Christ are not always easy to follow, but there are observable rewards in belonging to it.

Sometimes accepting Christ as King brings a basic change in perspective and in the use of our time. For instance, Neville found himself giving up the game of bridge. Of course, there is nothing wrong with playing bridge, but Neville had become almost addicted to it and was spending much of his life playing it. Bridge was his life, and so, when his life began to centre upon Christ the King, one of the effects was that bridge was dethroned. Neville found he had other things to do with his life.

Betty found that, when she became a committed Christian, one of the effects was to change the way she dressed. She had quite a collection of bangles, which continually tinkled and jangled when she wore them. You could hear her coming. But when she accepted Christ as King, she came to the conclusion that they were a provocative and attention-seeking form of dress, unsuited to and unneeded by a citizen of his kingdom, and so she abandoned them. It certainly did not make her any less attractive.

You may feel that bridge and bangles are pretty trivial

matters, and certainly other Christians might not have felt the same leading to dispense with them. By contrast, the changes initiated by membership of Christ's kingdom are often anything but trivial. This was the case, for instance, in the life of Billy, a former member of the Ulster Volunteer Force, who told me that before his conversion to Christianity he was actively involved in terrorism and had a dozen or so names of republicans on his death list. 'They would all be dead by now but for Jesus,' he said. 'When I became a Christian, Jesus not only saved my life; he saved theirs too.'

Perhaps in the interest of honesty it ought to be added that not all who reckon to become citizens of the kingdom of our Lord remain loyal to its laws. Obedience to Christ the King can be very demanding and difficult. Some find it just too demanding, just too difficult. Earlier we were thinking about Colin, who put the kingship of Christ before the continuation of the adulterous affair in which he was involved and in doing so saved two families. This sort of response does not happen automatically. I find myself thinking of Peggy, a regular churchgoer, a beautiful girl who was well thought of by the other members of the congregation to which she belonged. She read lessons at services and looked set to become a church leader. But then a senior executive in the firm where she worked became attracted to her and they started an affair, and he told her he wanted to leave his wife and live with her. I learned of it and pleaded with her to remember her Christian commitment. But in this case the temptation was too strong. The last time I saw her she had turned her back on her church and it was all too clear that Jesus was no longer her King.

Equally sad in my eyes is the story of Cynthia, who made a decision to be a committed Christian but then found that her smart circle of agnostic friends no longer wanted to have anything to do with her. They would cross to the other side of the street to avoid even speaking to her. Unhappily, her friends proved more important to her than her new-found faith. She too turned her back on her church and on her Lord.

Whenever this happens, our Lord allows it. As we saw in the last chapter, a genuine independence of spirit is a basic ingredient of the way of life in his kingdom. He wants our allegiance to be given freely and without coercion or not at all. So it is that there is no barbed-wire frontier fence around the borders of the kingdom of Christ. As its citizens, we can cross its boundary any time we choose. We are totally free and will always be so. This does not mean, however, that Christ's kingship represents anything other than ultimate reality both in and beyond this world. It just means that you and I have a choice to make.

The festival of Ascension Day echoes the proclamation of Jesus, 'All authority in heaven and on earth has been given to me' (Matt 28:18). It presents Christ as King. But having done so it leaves each one of us to decide for ourselves whether he is to *be* King. It is for each one of us to answer the question, 'Is Jesus *my* King? Or if we are honest about ourselves, have we actually selected a different king? We have to face the challenge of whether we are really prepared to put Jesus first or whether, even if we are theoretical Christians, there is, when it comes to the crunch, something in life that is more important than Jesus. Perhaps the acquisition of money or power or popularity is more important? Perhaps some sin or addiction or prejudice? Perhaps some other person? Perhaps our own self? For the 'kingdom of I' has always been a serious challenger to the kingdom of God in the wayward choices of humankind.

If I reckon to be a serious Christian, I need to rediscover Ascension Day as a very good time to renew my personal oath of allegiance to Christ the King. And because this is a book that aims to recall us to the principles of the ascension, there can be no better way of concluding this chapter than by quoting one of the many examples in our hymnbooks of pledges addressed to Christ the King. If we choose to do so we can affirm it as our own here and now.

Take my life. and let it be
Consecrated, Lord, to thee

Take my hands, and let them move
At the impulse of thy love…

Take my voice, and let me sing
Always, only, for my King…

Take my intellect, and use
Every power as thou shalt choose…

Take my heart, it is thine own;
It shall be thy royal throne…

Take myself, and I will be
Ever, only, all for thee.

Frances Ridley Havergal

Amen.

Chapter 5
A festival of mission

The second strand of ascension teaching at the end of Matthew's Gospel contains a call and a challenge to spread the gospel. Jesus says: '... go and make disciples of all nations, baptising them in the name of the Father and of the Son and of the Holy Spirit, and teaching them to obey everything I have commanded you...' (Matt 28:19). This commission follows logically from the claim of the ascension that Jesus is King.

If Christ's authority is supreme, and if his kingdom is the ultimate reality both in and beyond this world, then it must follow that those who are learning to live as citizens of that kingdom must also be learning about life at its fullest and best. Contrast the other 'kingdoms' in our fallen world, of which there are so many – the kingdom of greed, the kingdom of hate, the kingdom of fear, the kingdom of lust ... the list is endless. It does not require a great deal of thought to realise that these lead us away from life as it should be. Weak and confused as we are, we often make an attempt at multiple citizenship. Even quite serious Christians can find this happening. We can try, for instance, to have one foot in the realm where Christ is King, while the other is in a different one, perhaps the one in which our main energy is directed towards what we might call 'making a decent living'. We can easily find ourselves trying to serve not only the real God but the money-god too. One of the signs that this is so could be that we hate to hear sermons about the stewardship of money and can sometimes become quite angry at preachers when this is their subject. Our patient God allows it to be so – for a time at any rate – but Jesus warns us that this ambiguous allegiance cannot go on indefinitely. 'No servant can serve two masters. Either he will hate the one and love the other, or he will be devoted to the one and despise the other. You cannot serve both God and Money' (Luke 16:13). Ultimately, we have to choose our priority, choose our king. This is all part of the message of the ascension.

But Jesus goes further than this. Not only do we have to choose for ourselves but we have to help others choose also. If we know that Jesus is the absolute best, we cannot claim to love our neighbour if we are keeping our knowledge of him strictly to ourselves. If Jesus is both God and man, embodying as such the only real hope that our self-damaged world has, we betray not only him but humankind too, unless we are involved in the proclamation of his kingdom. Ascension Day is therefore a festival of mission.

We who claim to be Christ's people often fail quite pitiably to hear this challenge. I think for example of Cyril, an officer in his local church, who had worked as a civil servant for many years. He said to me, 'I pride myself that no-one at work knows I am a churchgoer.' I remember his words exactly – 'I *pride* myself'. Yet pride should have been the very last thing he felt. He was guilty of clear disobedience to the Christ who, before the ascension, gave his followers this charge: '...you will be my witnesses in Jerusalem and in all

Judea and Samaria, and to the ends of the earth' (Acts 1:8). That must surely include Cyril's office!

For some years I was involved in my diocesan scheme for post-ordination training. A group of curates would come regularly to my vicarage so that we could discuss the principles and practicalities of effective ministry. From time to time we would have a session on the subject of pastoral visiting. It is so easy for clergy to visit in a haphazard and unfocused way. We can do so without ever asking ourselves what the point and purpose of pastoral visiting should be. Thus we can find ourselves going from house to house having a cup of tea with Mrs Brown, a piece of Mrs Green's homemade slab cake and a chat with Mr Black about the local football team. It is all very pleasant, but it may well achieve little in the advancement of Christ's kingdom.

I used to share with my post-ordination group my conviction that our visiting-list should be divided into three roughly equal parts. It should take us on visits of *contact*, of *comfort*, and of *challenge*. The aim of contact visits is simply so that we can know people and they can know us. We want as many as possible to be aware that, if ever they need us, we are available. So, in a phrase I remember from my theological college, we should be prepared to 'leave ourselves hanging about' for some of our time. This is where Mrs Brown's teapot and Mrs Green's slab cake and Mr Brown's passion for the local football team come in. But pastoral visiting should also have the power to *comfort*. The world is full of people experiencing problems and hurts – sick people, lonely people, depressed people, anxious people, people facing bereavement or unemployment or financial difficulties or family problems. It is for such that we are commanded, '"Comfort, comfort my people," says your God' (Isa 40:1). This means much more than just having a sympathetic word. It means being a vehicle of the perspective, the strength and the power of the healing Christ, whom we are called to represent.

Then too there should be visits of *challenge*. If I am honest, I have to admit that I am severely tempted to give these a miss. My natural personal motto could easily be 'Anything for a quiet life'. But I have had to learn that quiet living and right living are not necessarily the same thing. For instance, when Peggy launched into the adulterous affair, described in the last chapter, I knew that I had to call at her home for a challenge visit. There was nothing enjoyable about it either for me or for Peggy, and it did not succeed in deflecting her from her course; but I would have betrayed her and the Lord had I not tried. Clergy who never offer a challenge may well end up by not offering much at all. 'In this world you will have trouble,' Jesus told his disciples (John 16:33). An untroubled ministry is almost a contradiction in terms.

There are various sorts of challenge visits. They should certainly include occasions when we seek to bring the basic message of the gospel to people who may not otherwise hear it. Some years ago I worked for a time with a Nigerian clergyman, whose name was the Reverend Ezekiel Ogunsusi. He came over from Africa for a year's experience as a curate in an English parish. Ezekiel taught me a great deal about challenging people with the gospel. He never missed an opportunity to do this. When he met someone in the street who remarked that it was a dark day, Ezekiel replied, 'It reminds me of the day when darkness covered the land for three hours after Jesus died on the cross for us!' The man to whom he said it told me about it later. I don't suppose he ever forgot. Or there was the occasion when Ezekiel was invited to present the cup that had been won by our local football team. It happened at a celebration organised by the club at a pub in our parish. I shall always remember his words to them. 'I am told you have scored many goals. That is good. But I must ask you: have you made salvation your goal?' Once again he took the opportunity to launch into the heart of the gospel.

Ezekiel's approach to mission may not be the right style for everyone. However, we cannot ignore the challenge to find our own style of witnessing. Although so far I have been writing about the clergy, the same challenge comes to all Christians. We are *all* called to make a real *contact* with the people around us, for they are all precious to God. We are also called to bring *comfort* where it is needed, for we are all members of the body of the healing Christ. And the message of the ascension reminds us that all who bear the name of Christian are called to be channels of the *challenge* of the message of Christ.

The average British Christian does not find any of this easily acceptable. Most of us instinctively feel some degree of sympathy with Cyril's desire to keep his Christian convictions strictly private. In fact, if we ourselves should become the targets of some sort of spiritual challenge from a stranger, we may well find ourselves leaping to the conclusion that we must be in the presence of a Mormon, a Jehovah's Witness or someone who is just plain nutty.

Many years ago, as a teenager, I was unexpectedly accosted by a young woman while walking down a street in Derby. 'Are you saved?' she asked me, right out of the blue.

Rather pompously, I replied, 'I am hoping to become a clergyman.'

She knocked this aside with a sweep of her hands and the words, 'Oh, that doesn't matter. Lots of clergymen are damned!'

The experience did not do me any harm, and I now think back to her with a degree of affection. But at the time I assumed that she must be a touch deranged!

Of course, you and I do not fancy giving this sort of impression. Yet Christ's challenge should ring in our ears: 'Go and make disciples … you will be my witnesses'. If we think that Mormons and Jehovah's Witnesses (and others who may be theologically more orthodox but still use similar methods) are wrong in their approach, our response should be to seek to do better, not to slump into doing nothing.

If we were travelling through a desert and came across somebody dying of thirst, while we ourselves knew where water was to be found, then, if there were any heart in us at all, we should of course pass on the information. Spiritually speaking, this is precisely the situation in which we find ourselves, if Scripture is to be believed. The only difference is that many of our contemporaries seem to have no notion at all of how spiritually dehydrated they have become. All around us we see in society a blend of supposedly scientific secularism along with some surprisingly non-scientific superstitions, all mixed in with a great deal of plain, old-fashioned sinfulness. This has become the order of the day, though many would think that describing it in terms of secularism, superstition and sin, as I have just done, is a sign of bigotry, because this pattern of life has become so generally acceptable. We tend to close our eyes and our ears to the danger of it all. But if we are to be caring Christians we must stop just being politely inoffensive. The biblical perspective is that communicating the gospel is a matter of life and death. James reminds us that it has always been so. 'My brothers, if one of you should wander from the truth', he says, 'and someone should bring him back, remember this:

Whoever turns a sinner from the error of his way will save him from death and cover over a multitude of sins' (James 5:19,20).

If perhaps, then, with some reluctance, we hear Christ's call and consider our own potential to be bearers of the gospel in this society, where the majority seem to have such a resistance to him – if we accept our role as emissaries of Christ the King in an alien land – what are the implications of this for our own lives? Mercifully, the principles and practicalities of a Christian emissary have been set out for us by no less a person than Jesus himself. We can find his own mission plan in the New Testament and particularly in Luke's Gospel.

Luke 8 contains details of a mission conducted by Jesus himself, in which both preaching and healing had a prominent place. Luke 9 tells us how he extended this to the twelve apostles. But it is Luke 10 that requires our particular attention. For it is here that we learn how Jesus then turned with the same commission to *all* the people who were currently with him as followers. There happened to be seventy-two of them. He could have wished that there were more, as he told them when he said that 'the harvest is plentiful, but the workers are few...' (Luke 10:2). But they were the ones who happened to be available at the time and so he used what he had. Without exception he sent them out to bear his message. Before they went out, he presented them with a ten-point mission plan, which has been preserved for us in Luke 10:1–9. It is well worth our while to look at each point, so that we can see how far they provide a basis for our own part in the Christian mission. Here is a list of them with a brief comment on each one.

1. *Make prayer the foundation of everything.* Do this, said Jesus, before you do anything. Pray not just for yourself and your own role but that Christians everywhere will hear the challenge to take part in the mission of Jesus. In his own words, 'Pray to the owner of the harvest that he will send out workers to gather in his harvest' (Luke 10:2, Good News Bible).

2. *Be prepared for trouble.* Jesus never allows his followers to be under the illusion that Christian outreach will be easy. In fact, his words are distinctly scary: '...I am sending you out like lambs among wolves' (Luke 10:3).

3. *Travel light.* Many of the original seventy-two did not have a purse or a bag or even decent shoes. But Christ sent them out just the same. In a materialistic world it constitutes a powerful silent witness if Christians are perceived to be less dependent on this world's goods than others. In the developing world today many Christians join in the mission of Jesus though they have as few possessions as the seventy-two had, and often they are gloriously effective. We who are part of western society and who share its material prosperity are often much less so. It is perhaps worth asking whether we tend to over-prepare and over-resource any attempts we make at mission.

4. *Have a sense of urgency.* Jesus tells the seventy-two not to waste time on idle chatter. He even goes as far as to tell them not to 'greet anyone on the road' (Luke 10:4). In Christian outreach we need to be clear about our purpose and its importance. We, like James, need to see mission as a matter of life and death.

5. *Wherever you go, take the peace of God with you.* There is so little of it in the world and it is so desperately needed. So 'When you enter a house, first say, "Peace to this house"' (Luke 10:5). If our presence can somehow communicate a sense of God's peace, this in itself will be a power for mission.

6. *If you are rejected, don't worry.* Free will is God's gift to humankind. It is a wonderful human attribute, but it is also highly dangerous. For we may use it or misuse it. Those to whom the gospel is offered are free to reject it. There will, of course, be negative consequences from this rejection, but Jesus says that this is not to be the concern of those who make the offer in his name, who may themselves go on their way, still retaining a sense of his peace. Peace 'will return to you', promises Jesus (Luke 10:6).

7. *Don't hurry.* Although the seventy-two are to have a sense of urgency, there is to be no sense of rush. If you are made welcome, says Jesus, be prepared to 'Stay in that house...' (Luke 10:7).

8. *Don't be too proud to be dependent.* Accept hospitality from those who offer it, 'eating and drinking whatever they give you...' (Luke 10:7).

9. *Don't be surprised if healing takes place when the gospel is communicated.* The church has been guilty of losing its grasp on the healing implications of our mission for Christ, but this is something that is being rediscovered in our time. The seventy-two are commanded: 'Heal the sick...' (Luke 10:9). We shall look at this later on, and also at the fact that for us it is a natural and logical consequence of the ascension.

10. *Proclaim the kingdom.* This is the overarching purpose of the mission of the seventy-two. Everyone they encounter is to be introduced both to Christ's kingdom and to its King. 'Tell them,' says Jesus, 'the kingdom of God is near you' (Luke 10:9).

It should be said that Christ's ten-point mission-briefing was given at a specific time and aimed at a specific situation. We should not assume we can transfer it, just as it stands, to our own day and age. But coming, as it does, directly from Jesus, we cannot afford to ignore its underlying principles.

We shall need to make some adaptations in the light of our own circumstances. For we cannot be true to the Lord unless we are also true to ourselves. We need to be sensitive and aware of the world around us and, if we want our neighbours to know what Christ can do for them, we must let them know what he has done for us.

Finally, I have not yet mentioned the best news of all, if we are prepared to take Christ's call to mission seriously. We are actually more fortunate than the seventy-two. They went out *for* Christ, but we are privileged to go out *with* Christ. They went out in his *service*, whereas it is part of the message of the ascension that we have the amazing honour of going out in his *presence*. It is to this revolutionary thought that we must now turn.

Chapter 6
The festival of the Christ who is with us

If I were to gather together a group of reasonably thought-ful Christians and ask them about the significance of the fes-tival of the ascension, my guess is that someone would speak about the kingship of Christ. Possibly, too, someone might just remember that, before Jesus ascended into heaven, he called his church to the task of worldwide mission. But I doubt whether anyone would make the link between the ascension and the miracle of Christ's presence with us now.

Yet for me, at any rate, the ascension is above all a celeb-ration of the Christian conviction that, when the followers of Jesus come together today, we not only meet one another but we actually meet *him*. This is Matthew's third strand of ascension teaching. It brings his Gospel to its triumphant climax and conclusion, as he records the uniquely precious words of Jesus: '... I am with you always, to the very end of the age', or, in the resounding translation of the old Authorised Version, '... lo, I am with you alway, even unto the end of the world' (Matt 28:20).

Here was something radically new in the experience of the disciples. During the earthly ministry of Jesus, he was present only in one place at a time. If he was walking the streets of Nazareth, he could not simultaneously be found in Jerusalem. If he was in Jerusalem he was not in Nazareth. If he was resident in his little house in Capernaum, he would not be found either in Jerusalem or in Nazareth. Even during the forty days of Easter, after he had been raised from the dead, we are not told of his being in more than one place at a time. So it was that Mary Magdalene was not allowed to cling to him when she discovered him in the sepulchre garden. For he had other places to go and other things to do. His words to her were, 'Do not hold on to me, because I have not yet ascended to the Father...' (John 20:17, New Revised Standard Version).

But after the ascension everything was to change, both for her and for all his followers. All the spatio-temporal restrictions were lifted at that point. From then on, wherever Christians were to be found, there too the Lord himself would be present. They had his personal guarantee. Each Christian can now echo the words of A H Ackley's hymn, 'He walks with me and talks with me along life's narrow way.'

In my study there hangs a remarkable picture. It used to hang on the wall in the sitting-room of the house of an elderly couple who lived in the parish where I first served as a vicar. They had bought it in a second-hand shop for just six old pence. But in spite of this derisory price they recognised a very special quality in it, and so did I. It shows Jesus with one of his disciples. Somehow it speaks uniquely of Jesus' presence and personality, and I was very moved indeed when the couple insisted on giving it to me when the time came for me to move on to my next parish. Since then it has always had an important place in my home, in my ministry and in my life.

The picture is the work of a remarkable Swiss artist named Eugene Burnand, who lived from 1850 to 1921; and, as I subsequently discovered, it was produced to commemorate a mission in the town of Basel. Burnand gave it the title *Suis moi* ('Follow me' – words that Jesus often spoke to those he called to be his disciples). The disciple in this picture could perhaps be John, because he resembles the figure of John in another of Burnand's pictures, *Les disciples Pierre et Jean courant au sepulcre* ('The disciples Peter and John running to the sepulchre') – capturing the moment when, having heard from Mary Magdalene about the resurrection, they hurried to see the empty tomb for themselves. I am happy not to know the identity of the second person in *Suis moi* for certain, however, because in my own prayers this figure has come to represent 'me', just as it can represent you. For it is to you and me that Jesus says, 'Follow me', today.

In the picture, with one of his hands Jesus points the way forward. His other arm is round the disciple's shoulder, giving strength and support. There are many signs of wilfulness and incomprehension in the expression on the face of the disciple, just as may well be the case with you and me; but Jesus himself was available to deal with this as far as the disciple in the picture was concerned, and that is precisely how it can be for you and me today if we claim Jesus' Ascension Day promise.

Think for a moment of your own situation and your own life. Wherever you happen to live, it is probable that near at hand there is a church of some sort. It may not usually be attended by a large congregation, but just imagine how that would change if it were suddenly to be known that, at one of the services next Sunday, Jesus himself would be present. There would be a real buzz around your neighbourhood, and next Sunday all sorts of people would turn up at the church to see just what he was like and what he would do.

'If only that could happen!' we say to ourselves. And yet, if we take Jesus' words before the ascension seriously, that is precisely what *will* happen next Sunday. Our purpose in going to church should not just be to experience the company of fellow Christians, with all that this can mean in terms of learning together, praying together and growing together. Good though all of this can be, our main aim should be an encounter with Jesus himself. The ascension brought with it the fulfilment of Christ's earlier pledge that 'where two or three come together in my name, there am I with them' (Matt 18:20). Christians today have a pressing need to rediscover this gospel message, as we come together Sunday by Sunday.

Back in the parish where I first discovered the artwork of Eugene Burnand, there was a village postmaster. He was regarded by many as a grumpy and awkward man. Indeed, I have to admit that that was exactly how I thought of him myself. Yet one day he did something very personal and special for me. I had gone into the post office to buy some stamps, and found myself saying how depressed I was feeling at the fact that our congregation was so small. He just looked at me without saying anything for a while and then he quoted Matthew 18:20 in the Authorised Version: '...where two or three are gathered together in my name, there am I in the midst of them'. That moment has remained in my mind ever since.

Of course, I ought not to have needed a reminder of the presence of Christ in worship. We sing about it often enough. For instance:

Jesus, where'er thy people meet,
There they behold thy mercy-seat;

Where'er they seek thee, thou art found,
And every place is hallowed ground.

William Cowper

Or, in the words of 'We love the place, O God' (a hymn by William Bullock and Henry Baker that is etched into the minds of vicars of my generation, because it was inevitably sung every time we were installed in a new parish):

It is the house of prayer
Wherein thy servants meet;
And thou, O Lord, art there
Thy chosen flock to greet.

Sometimes this presence was specifically linked to Christ's Ascension Day pledge, as when Bishop Reginald Heber wrote:

We thy parting promise claim
Assembled in thy sacred name.

Modern hymns are equally keen to celebrate our meeting with Jesus when we come together as Christians. Ranging from David Evans' 'Be still, for the presence of the Lord' to Graham Kendrick's 'Jesus, stand among us', we find that hymnbooks today take the presence of Jesus at the heart of worship as one of their major themes.

And if that is good news, there is even better. For when we leave our place of worship, we do not leave our Lord behind. It is his will, and since the ascension it is his promise and his practice, to be with every believer throughout every part of our lives. Once again, many a hymn is a meditation on this theme, not least Henry Francis Lyte's famous hymn 'Abide with me', which not only contemplates Christ's presence at the point of death but also celebrates his presence through-out the whole of life. At its heart are these words:

Who like thyself my guide and stay can be?
Through cloud and sunshine, O abide with me.

Once again the hymns we sing link this life-long presence of Jesus to his Ascension Day promise, as in the hymn by W Chatterton Dix, 'Alleluia, sing to Jesus':

Alleluia! not as orphans
Are we left in sorrow now;
Alleluia! he is near us,
Faith believes, nor questions how;
Though the cloud from sight received him
When the forty days were o'er,
Shall our hearts forget his promise,
'I am with you evermore'?

Not a few hymns speak of Christian life as a 'walk with Jesus'. This ought to be more than a metaphor for us, if we take the ascension seriously. It may come as a surprise to learn that some people in our own day make the claim that they have actually experienced the presence of Jesus, not just in some vague and spiritual sense, but in a way that has been visible, audible or tangible, or even all three.

In one of my books, *Finding Hope and Healing through the Bible*,[1] I have introduced several such people. They range from rather respectable people, such as a young executive and a senior clergyman, to others from the less respectable end of society, as was the case with many folk encountered by Jesus during his earthly ministry. Others also testify to such experiences. For instance, in his book *Breakout*,[2] Fred Lemon tells the story of an encounter with Jesus, while he was in prison for a violent crime. He reports that the encounter was visible and audible and that it changed his life. More recently, Chris Lambrianou has told a similar story in his book *Escape from the Kray Madness*.[4]

Such experiences may be less rare than we realise. People who have had them are sometimes reluctant to make them public in case anyone should doubt their sanity, but most of them are ordinary folk whose word one would not doubt in other matters. When recently I told some of these stories at a residential conference at which some eighty people were present, I was amazed to find that about a quarter of them came to talk to me privately afterwards, to say that they believed they had experienced a comparable encounter with our Lord. It may well be that there is someone known to you who has had a similar experience but has never ventured to speak about it.

I have to admit that I cannot claim to have had an encounter of this sort myself. Oh, I would dearly love to experience the presence of the Lord visibly, audibly, tangibly, but so far I have never done so. On the basis of Christ's Ascension Day pledge, however, I take it as a matter of faith that I can claim the real presence of Jesus as a basic ingredient in my life. If you are a believer, you can do so too.

This is a concept packed with implications, as indeed is the case for the whole of the Christian faith. All Christian doctrines have consequences, and if we fail to work them out, if we never ask, 'So what?', our personal religion can become a matter for the mind alone, bypassing the heart and soul, external, theoretical and powerless. We may well find ourselves merely cherishing orthodoxy or trumpeting slogans, without ever being changed in the process or having any real impact on the world in which we live. This is not how Christianity was meant to be, and it is certainly not how the ascension should be for us with its essential emphasis on the omnipresence of Jesus among believers.

His presence was never a non-event during the days of his earthly ministry. Those who responded to him were never the same afterwards. Even those who resisted and rejected him found that one way or another they could not be unaffected by him. And so it was that the early Christians discovered that believing he was truly with them from the ascension onwards had a profound impact on them and through them. For instance, Mark's Gospel says of the apostles: '... after talking with them the Lord Jesus was taken up into heaven and took his seat at the right hand of God; but they went out to proclaim their message far and wide, *and the Lord worked with them*.' The results amazed everybody. For Jesus 'confirmed their words by the miracles that followed' (Mark 16:19,20, Revised English Bible, emphasis added).

If the festival of the ascension affirms and celebrates the Christ who is with us – if, in Graham Kendrick's words, 'The King is among us' – how must this fact affect you and me? That will be the key concern of the rest of this book.

Chapter 7
A bridge to Pentecost

One of the most exciting things to happen in the churches during my years in the ministry has been the eruption of the charismatic movement on to the world scene. It has affected all the major Christian denominations.

Its roots are to be found in the Pentecostal meetings that began to be held in the early years of the twentieth century and that, so far as the British Isles are concerned, received a considerable boost between 1925 and 1935 from the ministry of three Welsh evangelists, Stephen, George and Edward Jeffreys. But it was not till the second half of the twentieth century that this movement spilled out from its Pentecostal beginnings and started to find a place in all the major Christian churches.

The movement's keynote was a greatly increased emphasis on the person, the work and the gifts of the Holy Spirit. It was characterised by a distinctive type of praise-worship, which often included speaking and singing in tongues and the offering of what were claimed to be prophetic words of wisdom and knowledge. It could be found in churches of remarkable diversity, High and Low, fundamentalist and liberal, Protestant and Catholic. Martyn Percy's assessment of the charismatic movement in *The New Dictionary of Pastoral Studies*[1] takes the view that, among the revivals that have taken place in the history of the church, the charismatic movement is arguably the largest and most global of them, perhaps influencing up to one fifth of the world's Christian population.

In the early 1970s I was invited by my bishop to go on a refresher course at Wycliffe Hall, Oxford, and found on arrival that both the college and much of the university seemed to be in the grip of charismatic discovery and activity. I went to a prayer meeting that began with forty-five minutes of spontaneous praise to God – no confession or intercession, but just continuous praise, much of it in tongues. Never before had I experienced anything quite like it. Back in my room on my own, I tried to work out my feelings about it all. I found myself musing not only on the prayer meeting but on the whole Oxford scene. I also found myself offering a quiet and deliberate prayer to God in which I told him that if, for some reason, he wished me to explore the charismatic phenomenon from the inside rather than merely being a spectator, *he* would have to do something about it, because I had absolutely no idea how to do it for myself. Retrospectively, it did not seem much of a prayer, but evidently it was enough. Suddenly and unexpectedly I found that prayer in tongues was flooding out of me. With it there came an extraordinary lightening of my spirit – along with a silly-looking grin, which I did not manage to lose for several days.

In the room next to mine was a Liverpool clergyman who was also undertaking a refresher course. He saw that something had happened to me and invited me in for a coffee, so that he could extract the details from me. When I had told him my story, he asked whether I would lay hands on him to see whether he could undergo a similar experience. I remember telling him that I had little expectation that a laying on of hands from me would have any effect on him at all. How wrong I was! Within moments of my touching him, prayers in tongues were gushing out of him too. Since then prayer in tongues has been a part of his personal devotional life and of mine. Now, decades later, we have both had a great deal of time to consider just what it was that happened to us. Readers who may be interested to know how I ultimately evaluated the phenomenon of praying in tongues can find my assessment in the epilogue to my earlier book *How to Pray when Life Hurts.*[2]

At the time, however, back in the 1970s, after a few weeks in Oxford I had to return to my church and immerse myself once again in the round of parish activities. I suppose that some might have called me a renewed person – and a renewed parson! Certainly, one effect of the experiences I had undergone was that I began to discover many new dimensions of life and ministry from then on. But in all honesty I have to add that before long I was also to discover that there were dangers as well as delights in the charismatic movement.

For instance, I was to learn that, though many found the exercise of charismatic gifts a joyful and liberating event, those gifts did not always seem necessarily to be rooted in reality. Libby and her husband Dick provided a painful example of this. They were on the receiving end of some decidedly dubious charismatic ministry. They had both been devastated when Dick was found to be suffering from a life-threatening cancer, but one of Libby's charismatic friends visited them to say that a 'word of knowledge' from the Holy Spirit had made her certain that they need not worry and that all was to be well with Dick. In fact, physically speaking, all was to be far from well with him. It was not long before he died. The charismatic friend then proceeded radically to reinterpret her 'word of knowledge'. Apparently, it now meant that, though Dick had not been a regular churchgoer, God would find a way for all to be well with him within the mystery of eternity. Please God that this is so. For Dick was a generous and friendly man whose company I often enjoyed. I would hate to think that all the good things in him had been eternally wasted. But, as far as the word of knowledge was concerned, does not this sort of change of interpretation look suspiciously like trying to have your cake and eat it?

It rather reminded me of how, back in ancient Greece, the authorities who ran the Delphic oracle would never admit to error and so predictions were regularly reinterpreted. So it was, for instance, when Croesus, who was king of Lydia from 560 to 546 BC, came laden with gifts to obtain guidance from the shrine. The purpose of his visit was to enquire whether or not he should launch an attack on the Persians. The response he received from the oracle was, 'If Croesus attacks the Persians, he will destroy a great empire.' Well pleased with this, he went into battle – only to be roundly defeated. In spite of this, no error was admitted in the prediction. It was explained that he had destroyed a great empire – his own! But surely a word of knowledge from God the Holy Spirit should be very different from that.

It would not be difficult for me to tell further stories of words of knowledge gone wrong, but this was not the only problem I was to encounter. Equally disturbing was the fact that I could not help noticing that in some charismatic churches painful and damaging divisions were developing. In some cases congregations were split down the middle. A great deal of ill will could be generated in such instances.

When it happened, one explanation that was sometimes offered was that one must expect new, living Christians to be opposed by fuddy-duddy traditionalists, who were more interested in preserving ancient and dead forms of worship than in genuinely seeking God's will. The battle, it was suggested, was between the renewed and the unrenewed, between those who rejoice in the Spirit of God and those who are hell-bent on opposing any fresh way in which he would move. But I could not help but feel that this was much too simplistic. For I could see from experience that the traditionalists included many whose love of God was deep and real, and I also knew that charismatics could sometimes behave in ways that were brash, presumptuous and insensitive.

Paul the apostle, whom many charismatics have virtually adopted as their patron saint because of his stress on spiritual gifts (see 1 Cor 12), was well aware that the lives of those who claimed to exercise spiritual gifts sometimes left a great deal to be desired. He taught that gifts of the Spirit require discipline and restraint in their use and suggested rules and guidelines because 'everything should be done in a fitting and orderly way' (1 Cor 14:40). He also taught that what are claimed to be such gifts should be regarded with a degree of suspicion unless they build up the body of Christ. For 'the manifestation of the Spirit is given for the common good.' (1 Cor 12:7). He further taught the need not just for the 'gifts' of the Spirit but also for the 'fruit' of the Spirit – 'love, peace, patience, kindness, goodness, faithfulness, gentleness and self-control' (Gal 5:22,23). Indeed, he went as far as to say that without the fruit of 'love' any spiritual gifts we may exercise will be worth absolutely nothing. 'If I speak in the tongues of men and of angels, but have not love, I am only a resounding gong or a clanging cymbal. If I have the gift of prophecy and can fathom all mysteries and all knowledge, and if I have a faith that can move mountains, but have not love, I am nothing' (1 Cor 13:1,2).

The scriptural perspective that emerges from all this is that, on the one hand, Paul clearly wants his readers to take God the Holy Spirit very seriously indeed. For he knows that to neglect the Holy Spirit will reduce the church to impotence and irrelevance. But, on the other hand, Paul is aware that those who would exercise a Spirit-filled ministry must walk across a minefield in the process.

What does this say to us today? How shall we manage to learn from the wide and sometimes confusing range of experiences of Christians past and present in their search for life within the power of the Holy Spirit? Where are we to find a path to Pentecost that you and I can take with confidence? My belief is that in order to find answers to these questions we must go, once again, to Christ as he presented himself to the disciples on the Mount of Ascension and to the fundamentals of faith he shared with them there.

It is a historical fact of the gospel that before the apostles could experience Pentecost they first had to experience the ascension. It was at the ascension that Jesus promised them, 'You will receive power when the Holy Spirit comes on you...' (Acts 1:8). Similarly, before Paul could receive the Holy Spirit, it was necessary for him to encounter the ascended Christ. This encounter was so important that it is recorded no fewer than three times in the Acts (9:3–5; 22:6–10; 26:13–18). This biblical sequence, which teaches that first we must encounter the living Christ and that only then shall we find that his presence will lead us into an experience of the fullness of the Holy Spirit, is just as applicable and just as available now as it was in the days of the early church.

You and I may not see the same 'blazing light from

heaven' that Paul saw, but it is as we encounter the Christ whose presence among us has been guaranteed since the ascension that the Holy Spirit can be stirred to new life in us. Let me try to lay a trail of texts from the New Testament to show just how prominent a scriptural principle this is.

It was John the Baptist who laid down the ground-rule that only Jesus can offer baptism in the Holy Spirit. He said, 'I baptise you with water. But one more powerful than I will come, the thongs of whose sandals I am not worthy to untie. He will baptise you with the Holy Spirit ...' (Luke 3:16). John the Evangelist endorses this judgement. He adds that it was not during the pre-ascension ministry of Jesus that his followers received the fullness of the Holy Spirit. Pentecost depended on what he terms the 'glorification' of Jesus. He says that Jesus made this clear in words spoken on the occasion of the Jewish Feast of Tabernacles:

On the last and greatest day of the Feast, Jesus stood and said in a loud voice, 'If anyone is thirsty, let him come to me and drink. Whoever believes in me, as the Scripture has said, streams of living water will flow from within him.' By this he meant the Spirit, whom those who believed in him were later to receive. Up to that time the Spirit had not been given, since Jesus had not yet been glorified.

John 7:37–40

John says that the full power of the Holy Spirit is to be derived from the 'breath' or life-essence of Jesus himself (John 20:22). Paul makes the same point. His alternative name for the Holy Spirit is 'the Spirit of Jesus Christ' (Phil 1:19) or 'the Spirit of Christ' (Rom 8:9). Peter also refers to the Holy Spirit as 'the Spirit of Christ' (1 Pet 1:11). It was because baptism was regarded as an incorporation into the life and essence of Jesus that Peter could declare: 'Repent and be baptised, every one of you, in the name of Jesus Christ for the forgiveness of your sins. And you will receive the gift of the Holy Spirit' (Acts 2:38). It is a fundamental Christian conviction that to be filled with the Holy Spirit depends upon the constant practice of the presence of Christ. The journey to Pentecost must take us first to the crib, then to the cross, then to the empty tomb and finally to the Mount of Ascension.

It is as we ponder the historical coming of Jesus at the first Christmas, his death upon the cross for us on Good Friday, his rising to life again at Easter and his Ascension Day pledge to be with us to the end of the age, that we find we are journeying to our own Pentecost. For Jesus was and is infectious with the Holy Spirit. To put this once again in the words of John the Baptist, after he witnessed the mysterious events at the baptism of Jesus in the River Jordan: 'The man on whom you see the Spirit come down and remain is he who will baptise with the Holy Spirit' (John 1:33).

'Jesus is the reason for the season.' We use these words as a Christmas slogan, but they are equally true of Pentecost. If we fail to set Pentecost against the background of *all* that Jesus has done for us from his birth on earth to his ascension into heaven, then both our concept and our experience of the Holy Spirit will be flawed and inadequate. Many may not regard this as welcome news in our day and age. For ours is an impatient society, addicted to shortcuts. These range from instant coffee to instant sex. So it would hardly be sur-prising if we have a fancy for an instant experience of the Holy Spirit. But we need to take care. There is no shortcut to Pentecost. If we do not take the Jesus route, we may end up confusing our own bright ideas or our own wishful thinking with the promptings of the Spirit. If we claim too readily that 'the Holy Spirit has said this or that to me', we may just end up by deifying our own preconceived ideas or pandering to our own emotional needs. We must always practise the presence of Christ before we seek to open ourselves to the Spirit and, equally, no matter how strongly we may feel that the Spirit has spoken to us, we must never fail to monitor and test this conviction by bringing it into his searching light. For if we fail to do this, it may just be that the *wrong* spirit will come to us.

So the ascension, with its teaching that 'The King is among us', is a bridge to Pentecost; and, as we shall now see, a bridge to much more besides.

Chapter 8
A promise of the final coming

Some time before I sat down to write this chapter, I was leading a Sunday service in a little church on the estuary of the River Dee. The congregation and I were sharing a Parish Communion service, and I found that the Scripture readings set for the day all dealt with the Christian conviction that, at the end of human history, as we know it, Jesus Christ will return to the earth as Judge and King. It was not surprising that this was the theme of the day, because there are over two hundred references to this doctrine in the pages of the New Testament. So anyone attending a church where the Scriptures are read in a systematic way, as is the case at Parish Communion, will find that this topic comes along automatically from time to time. You might therefore expect that Parish Communion sermons, which usually are based on the set Bible passages, would regularly deal with this subject.

Yet this is far from the case. What usually happens is that time and time again the clergy 'do a Nelson' as far as the final coming of Jesus is concerned. Having read their congregation a passage about it, they then put their preaching telescope to a blind eye and choose a totally different topic for their sermon. And this, in spite of the fact that the Nicene Creed, which the congregation will go on to recite after the sermon is over, contains the resounding claim that Christ 'will come again with glory to judge the living and the dead and his kingdom will have no end', and that as the bread and wine are consecrated all the people will be required to say, 'Christ has died, Christ is risen, Christ will come again.'

In that little Deeside church, on the spur of the moment, I decided to try some instant on-the-spot consumer research. Before beginning to preach, I asked the members of the congregation (who numbered perhaps a hundred that day) to put a hand up if during the past twelve months they had heard a sermon on the final coming of Jesus. Not a single hand went up. I extended the timescale and asked, 'What about the last five years?' Again not a single hand was raised. So I went for double or quits and said, 'What about the last ten years?' and then finally one single, solitary hand went up.

Here was an extraordinary thing. Though the final coming of Christ is a major Christian theme, which dominates Scripture in a way that few other doctrines do, and though this same theme is set prominently at the heart of the words of the services we share Sunday by Sunday, only one per cent of that congregation had heard a sermon that dealt with it during the course of a whole decade – and my guess is that this situation could be replicated in very many churches around the country.

As far as that particular congregation was concerned, I took immediate steps to try to fill the gaping hole I had discovered in the church's teaching programme. But why, I wonder, are preachers so often so unforthcoming, and indeed so positively chicken-hearted, in this area of Christian doctrine? Is it because we fear that people might be upset if we talk about the end of this era of human history? Or is it because we know that there are some distinctly outlandish sects that talk a great deal about the end of the world and we don't want to be thought to be like them? Or could it be that many of us who find ourselves in the pulpit of a church on Sunday have not actually worked out our own beliefs properly, as far as the last things are concerned?

We certainly ought to have worked them out. Not only is the final coming central in Scripture and liturgy, but it is a totally logical expectation if we believe in God at all. Just as the events in the stable at Bethlehem on the first Christmas Day are a logical consequence if we believe in a God who is all-loving (for Love must share itself with its beloved), so the doctrine of a further coming in power and glory, when this world order comes to an end, is equally a consequence of believing in God. For if God is not only all-loving but also all-powerful, then our sins and stupidities cannot be allowed to have the last word in his world. If God *is* God, then ultimately his will must prevail.

Another reason we should be working out our thoughts on the subject of the last things is that never before in the history of humankind has the end of the world, as we know it, been such a stark and cold scientific possibility. When I was a child, the world seemed indestructible. It is true that during the Second World War many dreadful things happened around the world. But the world itself did not seem to be under threat. In those days, if we came across someone carrying a sandwich board with the message 'The end of the world is at hand', we would have a little smile, assume we had met a crank, and go on our way undisturbed. But things are very different now. The continuance of life on earth seems distinctly fragile these days. There is a genuine possibility, some might even say a probability, that this era may come to an end very soon. We are rightly disturbed at the world's terrifying arsenal of weapons, both nuclear and some that seem even worse, with what is termed their 'potential for overkill', which means that there are more than enough of them to bring our species to an end. If a nuclear explosion does not do this, a disease explosion might do so. For the world is already being ravaged by deadly epidemics such as AIDS and other sexually trans-mitted diseases. We could fight these by changing our pattern of behaviour, but it looks as though we have no intention of doing so. Or it could be a major ecological dis-aster that will bring about our end. We are appallingly bad stewards of our planet and of the universe beyond it, and the more technically advanced we become, the more damage we seem ready and able to do.

If the Christian faith is relevant for all times and all possi-bilities, it must have something to say about these scenarios of possible self-destruction, and it must make sense for our ears and our minds to be open to whatever it has to say. What Christianity does say – and the Bible is very clear and specific about this – is that, if our time runs out here on Earth, either because of a disaster like the ones we have thought about or in some other way, God the Father will not just stand by and shrug his shoulders. He will intervene and, once again, he will do so through his Son, Jesus.

You may have noticed that personally I prefer to speak about the 'final coming' of Christ rather than about his 'second coming', which is the more usual phrase. This is because, if I read the New Testament rightly, it speaks of more than a twofold coming of Jesus into this world. The first coming was at the time of creation, when God the Son co-operated with God the Father in the making of the universe: '... without him nothing was made that has been made' (John 1:3), and '... all things were created by him and for him' (Col 1:16). We affirm this whenever we say the Nicene Creed: 'Through him all things were made.' And we sing about it in many hymns – for instance, in the words of Caroline Noel's 'At the name of Jesus': 'At his voice creation / Sprang at once to sight'; or Matthew Bridges' 'Crown him with many crowns', which describes Jesus as 'Creator of the rolling spheres, ineffably sublime'. When Jesus came as a little baby lying in a manger at Bethlehem, then that was his second coming.

Thirdly, as we saw earlier in Chapter 6, Christ now comes to you and me and all who seek to meet in his name and live in his service. This has been so for the past two millennia, ever since the ascension. But his final coming still lies ahead. Scripture tells us that it will be spectacular in the extreme, that to most of humankind it will be totally unexpected, that to those who set their hearts against God it will be unwelcome and unpleasant but totally irresistible, and that to those who seek to be the family and followers of Jesus the wonder and joy of it will be beyond our wildest imagination. For any who wish to know more about the Bible's teaching about the final coming of Jesus, there is an abundance of passages to which we can turn. They include Matthew 24,25; Mark 13,14; 1 Thessalonians 4; 2 Peter 2,3; and much of the book of Revelation.

The concept of the final coming was crucially important to Jesus himself. In fact, it is no exaggeration to say that he might not have been crucified if he had been prepared to deny his role at the end of time. Mark tells the story of how it looked as though his trial before the Sanhedrin could have totally collapsed, because the case against him was weak and the statements of the witnesses against him were mutu-

ally contradictory. But then by a stroke of perverse genius
the High Priest turned to Jesus himself with a direct question, 'Are you the Christ, the Son of the Blessed One?' (Mark
14:61). He must hardly have believed his luck when Jesus
sealed his own fate by replying, 'I am ... and you will see the
Son of Man sitting at the right hand of the Mighty One and
coming on the clouds of heaven' (Mark 14:62). With these
words he virtually signed his own death warrant

> *The High Priest tore his clothes. 'Why do we need any more wit-*
> *nesses?' he asked. 'You have heard the blasphemy. What do you*
> *think?'*
>
> *They all condemned him as worthy of death.*

Mark 14:63,64

How can you and I understand what it was that Jesus was
saying on that occasion and just why it was that he said it?
If we try to take the full weight of all the scriptural texts that
deal with the final coming into our minds, we may find they
are too much for us. For these texts employ many styles and
idioms and take us into dimensions of thought and imagination well beyond our limited capacity. But there is one
place to which we can go in Scripture where the final coming
falls into perspective. Once again we must visit the Mount
of Ascension.

We are told in the Acts that, after Jesus had spoken his last
words and had been received into a cloud away from the
sight of his disciples, quite suddenly 'two men dressed in
white' appeared, standing beside them (1:10). This is a term
Luke uses to describe angels (see also Luke 24:4). Just as he

records that angels were available to explain the significance of the coming of Jesus on the first Christmas Day (Luke 2:8–14), so now he records that angels were available on Ascension Day to help the disciples understand his departure.

There were all kinds of things they might have said on that occasion, as the disciples strained their eyes for some lingering trace of the Lord who had just gone from their sight; but according to Luke at this moment they chose to focus the minds of his followers on the fact that the ascension of Jesus into heaven provides a guarantee for them and us that he will return:

> *'Men of Galilee,' they said, 'why do you stand here looking into the sky? This same Jesus, who has been taken from you into heaven, will come back in the same way you have seen him go into heaven.'*

Acts 1: 11

The more we think about these words the more we can see that the final coming of Jesus follows naturally and necessarily from his ascension into heaven. Just as we saw earlier that if God is God, human sin and stupidity cannot have the last word in the history of planet Earth, similarly if the ascended Christ is truly King, it is logical that he will play his part when the events of the last days take their course. His kingship must ultimately become not just a matter of faith but a matter of incontrovertible experience. If Jesus is God the Son, sovereign over heaven and earth, then in the fullness of time every knee *must* bow before him, either willingly or unwillingly.

So how does it affect you and me, this concept of the Christ who will come again in power and great glory to judge both the living and the dead? If, mixed in with other reactions, we feel a degree of fearfulness, perhaps this is understandable. For though you and I may seek to be followers of Jesus, I would guess that even the best of us can claim to be only a partial disciple. Our world is in a state of spiritual warfare, and you and I are part of the battlefield. There is some enemy-occupied territory in each one of us. Paul grieved over this state of affairs in himself and wrote about it with extraordinary honesty (see Rom 7:14–25). We too ought to admit that, though we can know that the powers of darkness cannot achieve ultimate victory if God is God, it is a matter of experience that these forces can show extraordinary tenacity in the incursions they make into our souls. Even in the best of us there is something that can identify with the biblical warning, 'It is a fearful thing to fall into the hands of the living God' (Heb 10:31, Authorised Version).

It was C S Lewis, in his book *The Problem of Pain*,[1] who pointed out that there is a parallel of sorts to this in Kenneth Grahame's children's story *The Wind in the Willows*, where, as Rat and Mole approach Pan, they find themselves speaking of the contrasting feelings they are experiencing. Mole finds himself trembling with emotion:

'Rat!' he found breath to whisper, shaking, 'Are you afraid?

'Afraid?' murmured the Rat, his eyes shining with unutterable love. 'Afraid! Of Him? O never, never! And yet – and yet – O, Mole, I am afraid!'[2]

They experience what could be described as a type of fearfulness, and yet with it there is a love that is much greater than their fear. This is a tiny indication of how it will be with you and me, when we stand at the last before Christ our cosmic King.

How then should we react, here and now, to the doctrine of the final coming of Christ? It is perhaps worth saying that we should not do as some Christians have done and waste our time playing 'the end-of-the-world date game'. Jesus made that much crystal clear on the Mount of Ascension, when he told his disciples, 'It is not for you to know the times or dates the Father has set by his own authority' (Acts 1:7). But, while leaving the countdown to the end of our era in the hands of God, there are certainly all sorts of things that we should be liberated both to feel and to do, as we ponder the implications of the final coming for our life today. For one thing, in a world like ours, where there are so many justifiable reasons for doom and gloom, it is all too easy to find ourselves paralysed by depression. If we believe in the final coming of Jesus, however, we have an antidote to that sort of depression, one that is rooted in the nature of God himself.

Even though Paul believed that terrible things would happen when human history draws to its close, he had no doubt that his doctrine of last things should be a source not primarily of fear but of strength and encouragement, as far as Christians are concerned. After writing about the return of Jesus, complete with archangel's shout and God's trumpet call, he adds, 'Therefore *encourage* each other with these words' (1 Thess 4:18, emphasis added). The older (Authorised) version of this text read '… *comfort* one another with these words'. For the concept of the final coming is good news, and when we are depressed by the many ways in which this world is damaged by the mistakes and misdeeds of humankind we can find deep comfort from the

Christian conviction that not one of the products of human wrong-headedness and wrong-heartedness will endure. By contrast, the things of God and the people of God will last for ever. Christ the King will see to it, when he comes again – or, in the words of Paul, 'The one who calls you is faithful and he will do it' (1 Thess 5:24). And if we are to take comfort we should also take *courage*. When the power of evil rears its head in the world, Christians should not cringe or cower before it, not if we have taken hold of the gospel promise that, no matter how things may appear in the short term, ultimately Christ must triumph.

The Christian martyrs of the apostolic age understood this well. Christian martyrs still do. For here and now, all around the world in the twenty-first century (even though we often allow this fact to slip from our minds), men, women and children are suffering for their faith in Jesus. In fact, according to statistics provided by Christian Solidarity Worldwide, every three minutes a Christian faces martyrdom somewhere. It seems that today's persecuted church both knows and shows the courage you and I are being called to rediscover.

Finally, there is one further rediscovery we are called to make. If we take comfort and courage from the promise given to the disciples on the Mount of Ascension that 'this same Jesus will come again', we can also take a new sense of *authority* as we go into society on his behalf. We British Christians are sometimes curiously apologetic for our faith. This cannot be appropriate. Ambassadors have always been required to hold their heads high and to speak with authority. For the one they represent speaks through them.

In this often hostile world, in which the voice of evil is so strident, ambassadors of Jesus should speak with a quiet authority. For our voice should be the voice of the one who not only is the ascended King but who one day, in fulfilment of the angels' promise, will return and prove it.

We are called to a confidence which is firmly built on the conviction that

Brothers, this Lord Jesus
Shall return again,
With his Father's glory,
With his angel train;
For all wreaths of empire
Meet upon his brow,
And our hearts confess him
King of glory now.

Caroline Noel

Chapter 9
The heart of prayer

Picture the scene. Jesus had just ascended into heaven. The eleven remaining apostles had heard his last words and seen his mysterious departure. Angels had appeared to them and had told them of those even more mysterious events that were yet to happen at the end of our era. And they now found themselves in something of a mental and spiritual daze as they came down from the Mount of Ascension and returned to the upper room in Jerusalem, which had become their home. There they met Mary, the mother of Jesus, and his brothers and those brave women who somehow had found the courage to remain by the cross after most of the men had run away.

I wonder if you can call to mind just what it was that they did next in the hours and days that immediately followed the ascension. It was something they were to do together again and again, something that was to become a regular activity in the life of the early church, and something Luke was determined that his readers should know and explore for themselves. What they did was to *pray*. 'They all joined together constantly in prayer ...' (Acts 1:14).

Over the centuries, prayer has continued to be a fundamental ingredient of Christian life. Even those whose personal Christianity is little more than skin deep often find
themselves turning to prayer, if life becomes hard. For many
today, however, and especially for those who are part-timers
in prayer, very often this process involves little more than
making out a sort of shopping-list, which we take to the
celestial supermarket in the hope that God will have our re-
quisites in stock and may even allow a few freebies to come
in our direction. Or to put it another way, prayer can seem
like trying to press the right buttons on the cash machine
outside God's bank of blessings, in the hope that out will
come some 'pennies from heaven'.

What the disciples did was totally different from that. It
was integrally related to the promise that they had received
from Jesus before his ascension. They had been promised
that access to the presence of Christ the King would be their
privilege from that point on for as long as time would
endure. And so for the first disciples prayer was simply the
exercise of that privilege. It was their way of access to his
throne room, an access which is still available to you and me.
Thus the writer to the letter to the Hebrews can urge, 'Let *us*
then approach the throne of grace with confidence ...' (Heb
4:16, emphasis added). Changing the metaphor but staying
with Hebrews, we are told that 'The Son is the radiance of
God's glory ...' (Heb 1:3). So, if you will forgive the pun, we
can think of prayer as time spent 'Son-bathing', as we strip
ourselves off in the presence of Jesus and allow ourselves to
be permeated by his warmth and light.

I love the story of the old countryman who used to call in
at his local parish church and sit there for quiet prayer. He
would spend at least a few minutes doing this, and some-

times much longer, and he did it day after day for years. A new vicar came to the parish and was curious to know just what the old man had spent so much of his time actually doing during all these visits to the church. So he asked him, 'What do you say when you pray?'

'Not a lot,' came the reply. 'I just looks at him and he looks at me.'

That is the heart of Christian prayer. Put at its most basic level, it is simply being with Jesus. It is acknowledging and experiencing the presence of the King who is among us. If this is true and if, in the words of Hebrews, we may 'approach the throne of grace with confidence', how should we feel and behave as we do so? May I offer two contrasting options, two possible role-models? One is based on my own reaction to royalty. The other comes from one of my former parishioners, a lady whom we can call Gladys.

Let's start with me. I have to admit that, on the few occasions in my life when I have been invited into the presence of a member of the Royal Family, I have taken some trouble to behave with what I took to be suitable decorum. I have acquired a copy of *Debrett's Correct Form* and have consulted it carefully to make sure that I knew the proper forms of address and other matters of etiquette. In short, I have generally minded my Ps and Qs, and so the whole thing has hardly been a relaxing experience.

I guess that very many people would feel the same way, but not everyone – and certainly not Gladys. Gladys seems to have the knack of behaving totally naturally if she comes across one of the Royal Family. For instance, some time ago the Queen and Prince Philip came to visit our local hospital, and it became known that their route there would take their car right through the middle of our parish. So Gladys set up a row of chairs outside her front door, so that she and her mother and her granddaughter Ivy, and any of the neighbours who wanted to join them, could sit there and wave Union flags as the royal car drove past.

'It's a waste of time,' I told her. 'The car will be driving so quickly that you won't see much and there's no chance at all that the Queen will see you.'

How wrong I was. Maybe the royal programme was ahead of schedule. But whatever the reason, the car travelled quite slowly through our parish. When it came level with Gladys' row of chairs it actually stopped, and to everyone's surprise the Queen lowered her window.

Like a flash, little Ivy, who had been given a posy to hold, ran across the road and handed over her flowers with the words, 'Here y'ar, Queen!'

Gladys puffed across behind her, full of embarrassment, and started to apologise – only to find that Granny had followed her and had put her head through the car window, asking Prince Philip, 'Is nobody speaking to you, luv?' They all had a chat before the car moved on. And it was not long before Gladys was to meet Prince Philip again. Because of work she had done for the Children's Society she was invited to an event at Buckingham Palace. After walking round the rooms that had been opened up to the guests, Gladys found a sofa to sit on.

'My feet are killing me,' she said to a man who was standing nearby.

'Mine too,' he said. Once again it was Prince Philip.

If you are looking for a role-model for entering the presence of Christ the King, my suggestion is that you go with Gladys, sore feet and all, rather than with me and my copy of Debrett. For one of the basic rules about coming into the presence of Jesus is that he wants us to be ourselves. Our prayers will be of very little use to him or to us if we approach him with artificial language and stuffy pseudo-piety. In the words of Charlotte Elliot's hymn, when you and I approach Jesus, our motto has to be, 'Just as I am, I come.' He offers his real presence to us and in return he expects us to offer our real presence to him.

Have you come across the acronym WYSIWYG? Pronounced 'wizzywig', it is one of the mass of strange, gobbledegook terms you encounter in computer circles, and is short for 'What you see is what you get'. It means that the display on the computer screen looks just like the printed-out version. Jesus wants you and me to be 'WYSIWYG people' when we approach him in prayer. He wants us to be able to tell him with absolute truth, 'What you see is what you get.'

If there are elements in our lives which make us feel guilty and ashamed, therefore, we must bring our guilt and shame to him. If we have been hurt and our experience of life is making us depressed and angry, again we must not try to conceal it, not even if we should feel, as Job did, that the cause of our depression and the target of our anger might well be God himself! If we are anxious and afraid, Jesus wants us to be honest about our insecurity and mental pain. If we are in the grip of jealousy or envy, he wants us to come clean about it. I have written about all this in much greater detail in *How to Pray When Life Hurts,*[1]and so will not repeat its contents here. But I do have an additional thought to offer you at this point. Just as we are multi-faceted people and Jesus wants us to bring each one of those facets to him, so he is a multi-faceted Saviour and he calls us to explore as many of his facets as we can take in.

Hebrews says that we should come to him on his throne, where he reigns as King; but it also says we should come to him on the cross, where he hung to become the Saviour of the world. '... Jesus ... suffered outside the city gate to make the people holy through his own blood. Let us, then, go to him outside the camp, bearing the disgrace he bore' (Heb 13:12,13). Every part of the life and experience of Jesus represents an eternal truth. For he is 'the same yesterday and today and for ever' (Heb 13:8). So everything that he has shown to us and done for us can be part of our prayer-relationship with him. We can come to Jesus the Teacher, Jesus the Healer, to Jesus who knew about family life because of his home life at Nazareth, to Jesus who was willing to meet all and who rejected none. We can come to the boy Jesus, the adult Jesus, the dying Jesus, the risen Jesus, the ascending Jesus, to Jesus as our King, our Lord, our Saviour, our Friend, our Companion along life's road. We can come to him as Son of Man. We can come to him as Son of God. All this can be part of the daily friendship with him, which is the heart of Christian prayer and which should be as rich and varied as we are and as he is. It is from this friendship, which stems from the access to his presence that all believers have had the privilege of enjoying ever since the ascension, that all the other classical ingredients of Christian devotional life can naturally flow – adoration, confession, thanksgiving, intercession, petition and much more beside.

All the persons of the Holy Trinity will be involved in this encounter with Jesus. We have already seen, in Chapter 4, that the throne of Christ the King is set at the right hand of God the Father. When Jesus taught his followers about prayer, he took them straight into his Father's presence (Luke 11:2). In fact, he said that you could not see him without also seeing his Father (John 14:9). Similarly, he taught that those whom he leads to the Father will find the Holy Spirit moving in them. They have only to ask (Luke 11:13). At Pentecost this became the experience of the disciples just as Jesus had promised at the ascension (Acts 1:8). It will happen to us too, if we approach the Father through him. So it is not just baptismal prayer that is offered 'in the name of the Father and of the Son and of the Holy Spirit' (Matt 28:19). The whole experience of Christian prayer is Trinitarian. To put it in the traditional way, it is offered 'through' the Son, 'to' the Father, 'in' the Spirit. And prayer is never a non-event.

One of the congregation in my last parish very properly corrected me when I said to her, 'We'll say a little prayer.'

'Oh no, we won't!' she replied. 'There is no such thing as a "little prayer". Every prayer is a big prayer!'

How right she was.

Prayer is not just holding up a shopping-list to heaven. Yet, having said that, our Lord delights to meet the needs of his people and, through them, the needs of the world. I wonder if you noticed that, earlier, when we were thinking about the words from Hebrews about approaching the throne of Jesus, I quoted only half a text. It is time now for it all. 'Let us then approach the throne of grace with confidence, *so that we may receive mercy and find grace to help us in our time of need*' (Heb 4:16, emphasis added).

This could bring us very neatly to the subject of our next chapter. I have a long-standing conviction, however, that one should never write about or read about the theory of prayer without stopping and actually doing some praying. The principles of prayer should never be divorced from its practice. Therefore, before we move on, here for your exploration is a method of prayer which I call 'Through all the changing scenes of life'. Be warned! Because it is based on the practice of the presence of Christ, it is an interactive process. It involves a number of searching questions, which you will be invited to put both to yourself and to him. Not all the answers may be as you expect and not all will come to you immediately – though more may come to you than you might expect. In the name of the Father and of the Son and of the Holy Spirit, then, here we go through all the changing scenes of life – with Jesus!

Any life that runs through a full span of years can be divided into seven main stages:

1   First there is childhood.

2   Then the transitional teenage years, which lead us to…

3   our early years as adults.

4   After that we come to what is sometimes called 'the prime of life', when hopefully we have found and are fulfilling our chosen role in the world.

5   Next there is a period when, though past our prime, we are still working hard to fulfil this role.

6   Then follow our years of active retirement, which ultimately bring us to our final stage…

7   the 'departure lounge' of this life, where we await and then experience death.

It is perfectly possible just to stumble through these seven stages without ever considering where we are going and what we are doing, but to do this is to risk total waste. It is better to have a goal and a direction and to consider them both regularly during the course of our journey through life.

For the Christian the whole experience should be a journey with Jesus. The ascension pledge reminds us that it is our privilege to claim his presence and to travel with him as our companion. Prayer is the monitoring process by which we check whether or not we are on course. It involves many a quick glance at Jesus day by day, and occasionally it requires something more detailed and extensive, a survey of life in his presence, a quiet time in which we lay other concerns aside and listen for any personal word that he may have for us. The prayer method which I now invite you to try out is one way of attempting such a survey. To facilitate its use, I have numbered its main stages.

First, remember and claim the promise of Jesus: 'I am with you always' (Matt 28:20). Picture yourself and him together. You look at him and he looks at you. His gaze is uncomfortably searching but also infinitely loving. Into that gaze, slowly and deliberately, bring each of the seven stages of your life, whether they are in the past, present or future.

1. Begin your self-exploration by mentally going back into your childhood, including your very earliest memories. This may require courage. For we may discover pains and traumas in the process. These were days of high dependency. They were also days of great significance for our subsequent development. In the presence of Christ, think about the input you received from your parents and from other family members, from schoolteachers and from the children who grew up with you, whether they were friends or far from friendly. Did this input equip you for life or did it do quite the opposite? What were the things that gave you pleasure? What were the things that caused you pain?

As your mind goes back to those early days, hopefully you will discover some real delights, but probably you will also unearth hurts and traumas. In either event, remember that this prayer method does not require you to travel back into those early days on your own. You are taking Jesus with you. He is holding and cherishing the child in you, and as he does so he offers you new strength and security, new insight both into yourself and into those who were involved in your life at that time.

It is worth saying that for some people this exercise may not be possible without help. For instance, those who have suffered some form of abuse in childhood may not be able to face up to the memory of it without the assistance of a skilled counsellor. Many clergy are now trained to give this sort of help. Even if you were not the victim of what can properly be termed abuse, there could still be inner problems, rooted in the past, which are best faced in the company of a trusted friend. Christians are certainly meant to help each other in this way. Paul says, 'Carry each other's burdens, and in this way you will fulfil the law of Christ' (Gal 6:2). But it is important that both you and any friend you may involve know well that our resource for facing past hurts lies in the practice of the presence of Christ. It is his love, his wisdom and his power that enable us to revisit those past events, which otherwise would fester beneath the surface of our consciousness and diminish our chances of living a happy and effective life here and now.

Even in the company of Jesus, we sometimes need real bravery to make the journey back into the past. But our ascended King will not fail us: he 'has gone into heaven and is at God's right hand – with angels, authorities and powers in submission to him' (1 Pet 3:22). If angels, authorities and powers quail before him, our fears have no chance of defeating him. Ultimately, there is no memory that you and he cannot face together.

2. Now move on to the teenage years. Let the main events of these years come back into your mind. What were the main influences that you experienced? Perhaps the power of peer pressure? Or the way you coped or failed to cope with sexual stirrings? Perhaps your first urges to be more independent of your parents? Perhaps feelings of rebellion against home and school and society? Recollect the first thoughts you had about and the first moves you may have made towards a career in life.

As you remember these things, continue to practise the presence of Christ. It may be helpful to bring your recollections and the feelings they engender in you now to the teenage Jesus, who did not always get on well with his family and whose parents did not always understand him (see Luke 2:50), but who still was a good son in these years of mental and physical development (Luke 2:51,52). Once again, allow yourself to be conscious of the things that helped you and the things that hurt you during this stage in life. If you now allow Jesus to become part of the peer pressure, does it influence the way in which you react to these years?

3. Next, move with him to your early adult years. Remember the hopes and fears that they contained. Remember your first experience of working life. What decisions did you have to make? Did you handle them rightly or wrongly? Can you now offer these years to Christ without shame or regret? If not, take this opportunity to ask and receive his forgiveness. For he is the Saviour who loves to say yes. If you are still in this period of life, check how far you are accepting Christ's guidance here and now. Check also that you are placing the future in his hands.

I will always be grateful for the advice I received as a young adult at a Christian conference: if I thought it likely I would at some point marry, I should there and then adopt the prayer-practice of regularly asking God's blessing on the woman who would eventually become my wife, whether at that stage I knew her identity or not. So I started to do exactly that, and sometimes I wonder how much the strong and lovely marriage my wife and I now share together may owe to the spiritual credit balance that those advance prayers helped to build up.

4. Next in your prayer review, turn to thoughts about the prime of life. Christ's own life on earth did not extend beyond his prime. 'The one who died upon the tree was but a man of thirty-three.' But of course the wisdom of the Son of God goes far beyond the experience of his earthly years. If, as you ponder your own prime of life in prayer, you are thinking back to a time in the past, let your mind recollect all the principal events and ingredients of these years. For many, these will be inseparable from the experience of marriage and of the birth and upbringing of children. If that is so for you, how do you now assess the experience that this involved for both you and your family? Do you now think that you brought up your children well? Bearing in mind that these are usually years during which you find yourself shouldering much more responsibility than before, how do you think you coped with it both at work and at home? Do you feel that you had the balance of life right? If not, is there something you should be doing about it now? Someone you should ask for forgiveness? Some relationship you should seek to mend?

If you are still in your prime, how well are you coping here and now? Or, if these years are as yet in the future for you, how are you preparing for them? To what extent are you placing the issues of these years in the hands of Jesus?

5. Next, what about the years when we soldier on with our main role in life, although by now we are past our prime? These are sometimes called 'the plateau years', because the odds are that, career-wise, by this stage in life we have arrived at whatever is to be our destination. At this stage it dawns upon us that we are not going to be field marshals or archbishops or captains of industry or international stars or whatever our dream may have been. The way we are is the way we are likely to remain. So we find ourselves asking, 'Is this it? Is this all there is to life?'

The advent of this stage of life can often bring with it a feeling of anticlimax and depression, and yet it is important to know that these can be truly good years. They can be significant and highly productive in terms of our development as human beings. For it is at this time that we may stop asking, 'What am I doing in life?' and start asking, 'What am I *becoming* in life?' The big question can now be not '*What* am I?' but '*Who* am I?' It may now finally strike home that what we do is less important than whether or not we are growing into the person God made us to be. We may also realise that our own development is integrally bound up in whether or not we are helping those who are around us to become their own best selves.

These are questions we can best explore in the presence of Jesus, and if we are wise we shall already have started to ask them long before we find ourselves in the plateau years.

Along with these fundamental issues, this is a time of life that brings with it a new selection of practical matters with which we have to grapple – for instance, those generated by the increasing intergenerational tensions, which can come along at this stage – as we find ourselves hassled by up-and-coming whiz-kids at work and by new practices in society. It has always been so. People in the second half of life have always been tempted to look at the past through rose-tinted spectacles and at the present and future through jaundiced eyes. I am told that the oldest inscription in the world, written in Babylonian cuneiform script, says when translated, 'Things aren't what they used to be!' So let Jesus govern your sense of proportion, at this and every stage.

6. And so to the years of retirement. These may be many years away in the future, as you undertake this prayer exercise. Or they may be just around the corner. Or you may already be there, as I am myself. How do you regard them? Do you see life as opening out or as contracting at this point? Is there a window of opportunity here or just a blank wall? What does Jesus say to you about the retirement years, as you practise his presence?

On the positive side, there are many new opportunities that can be both perceived and grasped, because of the new freedom retirement brings. How can this freedom best be used? On the negative side, there could be physical restrictions. There could be bereavement. Of course, both ill health and bereavement may be experienced at a much earlier stage of life too. What does Christ have to say to us about both? And what resources are available to us through his presence? Be still and listen for his voice.

7. Now we come to that time that sooner or later must come to us all, when we will realise that death is just around the corner. How shall we react to that experience? In fact, how do we react to the thought of it now? We can choose our own motto for dying. Will it be 'The party's over' or 'The best is yet to be'? We shall return to that question at the end of this book, but for the moment it is perhaps sufficient to remind ourselves that there are no spatio-temporal boundary posts in the realm of Christ the King, and, for those who travel with him and for him, the moment of physical death is just part of the journey.

The secret of it all is to keep our eyes on him. If our eyes are just upon ourselves, as we contemplate the changing scenes of life, there could perhaps be a degree of psychoanalytical benefit in doing so; but we could also find ourselves merely indulging in navel-gazing for its own sake. That is not how it will be if we keep our eyes on the Lord.

You may have heard the story of the old man who used to tell people that he had been saved by having good looks. When anybody queried this, he expanded it by saying that the good looks that save are good looks at Jesus: 'Let us fix our eyes on Jesus, the author and perfecter of our faith...' (Heb 12:2).

Good looks at the good Lord – this is the essence of receiving life and health from Christ, and it is the essence of this prayer method. If we review the seven stages of our life with our eyes fixed on him, we shall emerge from prayer with a new wholeness, a new sense of his love, a new sense of proportion and repentance and resolve and direction, and a new conviction that, whether in time or eternity, the best is truly yet to be.

Chapter 10
The basis of Christian healing

In Chapter 7 we looked at the charismatic movement. I shared with you something of my own encounter with it and of my conviction that, for a balanced assessment of all that happened at Pentecost, we need first to revisit the Mount of Ascension. Now I want to invite you consider in a similar way the rediscovery of Christian healing, which has been a major element in the life of the churches during my own time in the ministry.

It is important to note that the charismatic movement and the ministry of healing are not necessarily interconnected. While it is true that there is a concern for Christian healing within charismatic churches, they have no monopoly in this. The ministry of healing can be found in churches of every shade, tradition and practice. Thus, for example, there are sacramental expressions of Christian healing that are markedly different from those based on charismatic gifts. There are also quiet, devotional ministries, with an atmosphere far removed from charismatic activity. There are many residential homes of healing, each with its own atmosphere and ethos – such as Burrswood in Kent, for instance, noted both for its High Church tradition and its strong medical connections. There are shrines and holy places. And there is an increasing tendency for the healing ministry to have a central place in the life and worship of ordinary churches, whether High or Low or middle of the road.

All the major denominations have been moving forward in the discovery and practice of this ministry. Recently, it has been my privilege to serve for six years as a co-ordinator and consultant for the growing numbers of healing advisors who now exercise an important role in the mainstream churches throughout the British Isles. Thanks to secretarial back-up provided by the office staff of the Acorn Christian Foundation I have been able to edit and distribute an annual directory of these advisors, containing their names, addresses, telephone numbers, email particulars and areas of responsibility. This directory was used to facilitate the production of the *Time to Heal* report,[1] which was presented to the Anglican House of Bishops in 2000, a publication that has stimulated further growth and development in the practice of Christian healing throughout our islands both as far as the Church of England is concerned and also in other denominations.

It has to be admitted that not all Christians are equally enthusiastic about the recovery of the healing ministry. This is partly because, when spiritual healing is misinterpreted and misdirected, teaching about it can clearly be dangerous. There are two opposing errors that the church has to avoid if Christian healing is to be effective. On the one hand false hope must not be offered, but on the other hand true hope must not be withheld. To have the balance right, both doctrine and practice must be soundly based. How is such a basis to be found?

We have already seen that the authority for this ministry comes from Jesus himself. We saw in Chapter 5 that, when

Jesus presented his own mission plan to his followers, healing and evangelism were set side by side in it. He instructed them: 'When you enter a town and are welcomed, eat what is set before you. Heal the sick who are there and tell them "The kingdom of God is near you"' (Luke 10:8,9).

It was when I was made to realise that Christian healing was an integral part of Christ's commission to his church that – with some reluctance – I found myself drawn into this ministry personally. I remember clearly how this process was initiated. At the time, many years ago, I was in a car on the way to a clergy conference that the Bishop of Chester had convened at the Hotel Metropole in Blackpool. Quite casually, one of the clergy in the car said, 'Have you noticed that Jesus hardly ever commands his followers to "preach" without adding "and heal"? I wonder why it is,' he continued, 'that, when we have two equally important commands, we are so lopsided in our obedience? Week by week we go to our pulpits and preach, and yet most of us behave as though the command to heal had never been given.'

I suppose that most of what people have said to me over the years has gone into one ear and straight out of the other, but every so often I am presented with what becomes a seminal thought for me. It enters my mind and starts growing, whether I want it to or not. The comment in the car on the way to Blackpool proved to be such.

Up to that point I had tended to recoil from the idea of spiritual healing. It seemed to me to be intellectually disreputable, to smack of superstition and hocus-pocus. So could it possibly be true that Jesus had given his followers a straightforward command to be involved in it? I found myself forced back to many an hour of Bible study, as I looked for an answer to that question. It took me some months to realise it, but in time I had to acknowledge that the answer was absolutely clear. Healing is a primary scriptural topic. In fact, it is no exaggeration to say that the Bible is basically a book about healing. I don't just mean bodily healing, though there is no shortage of references to that. But Scripture's concern is much wider than the physical. It is about the healing of the essence of our being. And it is relevant to us not only as individuals, but corporately too. The Bible is about God's will for our total wellbeing, and so it concerns itself with body, mind and spirit, with attitudes, relationships and lifestyles, with neighbourhoods and nations, and it does so within the context of both time and eternity. As a species we have damaged ourselves and one another and the world in which we live. God would have it otherwise, however, and Scripture records his plan for our healing.

In the opening words of Genesis, God is revealed as Creator. 'In the beginning God created...' (Gen 1:1), and all that he made was designed to be 'very good' (Gen 1:31). When humankind was stupid and sinful enough to try to 'be like God' (Gen 3:5), putting self instead of God at the centre of life, God did not abandon us. Our Creator now revealed himself as our '*Re*-Creator'. 'I am the LORD, who heals you,' he said to Moses (Exod 15:26). The Psalms point to the worship of God as a healing activity.

> *Praise the LORD, O my soul,*
> *and forget not all his benefits –*
> *who forgives all your sins*
> *and heals all your diseases.*

Psalm 103:2,3

The biblical philosophy of life, if accepted, increases our level of wholeness.

> *... fear the LORD and shun evil.*
> *This will bring health to your body*
> *and nourishment to your bones.*

Proverbs 3:7,8

It followed that, since Jesus came into the world to do the will and the work of God the Father (John 6:38), healing was also his will and his work. When he saw a crowd of people in need, 'he had compassion on them and healed their sick' (Matt 14:14). And as well as occasions of mass healing, there were many times when he responded to individual needs. This was a ministry at many levels. Lives and lifestyles were dramatically affected. We see it again and again. Recipients range from the mean and money-grubbing Zacchaeus, who was transformed into a repentant and generous follower of Jesus (Luke 19:1–10), to Mary Magdalene, from whom (we are told) 'seven demons had come out' (Luke 8:2). Relationships were sometimes dramatically transformed. This is what happened to Matthew, who had been a Roman collaborator, and Simon Zealotes, a freedom fighter sworn to assassinate collaborators. Amazingly, they found themselves as fellow apostles, brothers in the faith. Many healings were mental and spiritual, as in the case of deranged man in the graveyard (Luke 8:26–39). But many others were physical and covered conditions such as blindness (Matt 9:27–31), deafness (Mark 7:31–35), lameness (Matt 11:4,5), paralysis (Matt 8:5–13), fever (Matt 8:14–15), severe skin conditions (Matt 8:1–3) and much more besides. Jesus also made it plain that it was his will to continue his healing ministry through his church. My colleague in the car on the way to Blackpool was right: Christ's dual commission was 'preach and heal' (Luke 9:2,6). The early disciples were obedient and effective in the ministry of healing. As with Jesus, there were mass healings (Acts 5:12–16) and many individual healings (Acts 3:1–16; 9:32–43; 20:8–10; 28:8,9).

Jesus saw healing as a sign and an element in the coming of the kingdom of God (Luke 10:9). Isaiah had seen it in the same way centuries earlier (Isa 35:4–6).

James spelt out some of the practicalities of this for Christian congregations:

> *Is any one of you sick? He should call the elders of the church to pray over him and anoint him with oil in the name of the Lord. And the prayer offered in faith will make the sick person well; the Lord will raise him up. If he has sinned, he will be forgiven. Therefore confess your sins to each other and pray for each other so that you may be healed. The prayer of a righteous man is powerful and effective.*

James 5:14–16

All of this became plain as I studied the topic of healing in the Scriptures. But how could I know that the ministry of healing that so characterised the life of Jesus and the apostles was meant to endure? How could I be sure that it was not a divine dispensation that was given for that very special time in human history but was withdrawn when the apostles died? How could I know that the commission given to them applies to us also?

For the answer to this question we must go once again to

the words of Jesus before he ascended into heaven. The mission charge given to the apostles at the end of Matthew's Gospel is very clear in the scope of its application: '... go and make disciples of all nations, baptising them in the name of the Father and of the Son and of the Holy Spirit, and teaching them to obey everything I have commanded you ...' (Matt 28:19,20). This 'everything' certainly would have included the Christian healing ministry, which had been very firmly placed in the hands of the disciples (Matt 10:1). And to make this doubly clear, in Mark's Gospel the last recorded words of Jesus to his disciples before his ascension are that those who believe 'will place their hands on sick people, and they will get well' (Mark 16:18).

Perhaps, if I am honest, long before the fateful conversation on the way to Blackpool, all of this scriptural information was available to me at the back of my mind. I am sure that I knew about the healing ministry of Jesus and probably I also knew that he had placed this ministry in the hands of his followers. But it was information I had chosen not to access. Even when preaching about the healing miracles of Jesus, I had often tended to spiritualise them, to turn them into parables, so that, for example, when Jesus helped the deaf to hear I would urge my congregation to open their ears afresh to gospel truth. And as for Christ's commission to heal, I would have found myself speaking about Christian work in hospitals and in hospices.

When I was confronted with the challenge to be involved in the ministry of Christian healing, I found that all sorts of doubts and fears and questions flooded into my mind, some of them distinctly unworthy ones. 'Suppose I try it and fail horribly? What if nothing actually works? Will it damage the faith of my congregation? Will it damage my own faith? And will I look a fool for even trying?' And if those are somewhat disreputable considerations, there was also a more serious theological issue.

Even though I knew I could claim a clear gospel authority for involvement in Christian healing, I was much less certain what actual resources would be available to me to enable that ministry to have any chance of effectiveness. My difficulty was this. When I visit my GP, his resources are easy to see. He can call on the assorted products of many pharmaceutical companies in order to give me a prescription. He can arrange for the wide range of mechanical gadgetry in our local hospitals to be used to diagnose and treat me. And behind him stand the serried ranks of specialist consultants and other medical personnel who are employed by the National Health Service. By contrast, if somehow I find the courage to obey the gospel imperative to offer the ministry of Christian healing, *who will stand behind me*? For I cannot help knowing that in my own strength I can do precious little.

Once again, if I am to find an answer, I must turn to the teachings of our Lord before the ascension, and in particular to the pledge of the continuing presence of Jesus with which Matthew ends his Gospel. For this is the basis of Christian healing, just as it is the basis of so much else in Christian life and ministry. There is only one 'healer' involved in Christian healing and that is Jesus himself. If I have a right understanding of the traditional practices associated with this ministry, they are all methods of practising the presence of the healing Christ. The 'laying on of hands' is no more and no less than the body of Christ communicating the touch of Christ. 'Anointing' is a powerful symbol of our oneness with the one who claimed the title of 'The Anointed One'. For that is the meaning of both the Hebrew word 'Messiah' and the Greek word 'Christ'.

'Holy Communion' is the service at which we spiritually feed on Jesus by the sacramental use of the bread and wine, of which Jesus said, 'this is my body' and 'This is my blood' (Mark 14:22,24). The 'ministry of deliverance' is based on the conviction that, when we practise the presence of Christ, all those hostile influences that can come to us from the world, the flesh and the devil must retreat before him. The 'ministry of forgiveness', which has such an important part to play in Christian healing, stems entirely from the personal relationship we are privileged to have with the Lord Jesus, because he died for us and now lives with and for us. And 'healing prayer', as we have already seen, is the experience of being with him and bringing those whom we love to him, knowing that in his earthly ministry he never failed to increase the experience of wholeness of those who came or were brought to him in need, and that he is 'the same yesterday and today and for ever' (Heb 13:8).

I am aware that some individuals are fortunate enough to have special personal gifts that they can use as they exercise this ministry. These gifts may be natural aptitudes, rather like the gift I have always had for music, which has enabled me to sit down at a piano since I was a child and just play. They may be charismatic endowments, of the sort that Paul describes in 1 Corinthians 12. Or they may be professional skills, medical or otherwise. But none of these constitute the centre-point of Christian healing. The centre is Jesus. He himself is *the* supreme gift. Once again, we need to remind ourselves that to come to Jesus is to open ourselves to all the resources of the Holy Trinity, and it is important it should be made clear that these resources are the basis of the ministry offered at Christian healing services.

It may be helpful to suggest a few thoughts about these services before this chapter comes to an end. The idiom in which they are conducted should be whatever comes naturally to each local congregation. The motto for Christian healing (as for so much else in Christian life and ministry) should be, 'Do it as you can, and not as you can't!' Congregations that prefer a traditional form of worship can adopt a traditional format for healing services. Those who are happier with informal worship can be informal in their healing ministry too. High Churches will still feel High. Low Churches will feel Low. Charismatics will still be charismatics, but non-charismatics will not have to be so. It will not be the idiom that does the healing, but the Lord himself. The sermon will aim to communicate his reality and purpose. The prayers will practise his presence. The laying on of hands will, it is to be hoped, never be offered in an intimidating or manipulative manner, but will simply be a way of experiencing his touch. The issues and consequences of it all will be left trustingly in his hands.

In order to provide an example of how this might work in practice, consider the case of a local church in which the leaders decide to hold a monthly Christian healing service at a date and time when there would normally be Holy Communion. If Communion were to be retained as a setting for the healing service, what would have to change? Actually, surprisingly little. The structure would still be that of an initial act of preparation and penitence, followed by the reading of Scripture, expounded by a sermon, followed by prayers of intercession, leading into the sharing of God's Peace, followed by the consecration and administration of the bread and wine, which signify the body and blood of Jesus, followed by the final prayers and blessing. So the sermon would remain in the same place, as would the prayers that follow, though both would now concentrate on some aspect of God's will for our wholeness. There is

usually something distinctive and special about the atmosphere at healing services, but this is due not so much to new
forms and patterns of worship as to a blend of the sense of
need and the sense of expectation which are both character-
istic of these occasions.

The only new structural element would be likely to be the
insertion of a laying on of hands in the name of Jesus at some
point. There are two ways of doing this that I would personally recommend. One is that, immediately before receiving the bread and wine, worshippers are given the
opportunity of receiving this additional ministry. In
churches where people are used to moving forward to
receive the sacrament, the laying on of hands can be offered
either at the communion rail or at some point on the way
towards it, though it will be made clear that none are obliged
to experience this ministry unless they wish to do so. I
believe it is best if the ministrants who are appointed to lay
on hands do so in pairs, just as Jesus sent out his followers
in pairs for the mission of preaching and healing, which is
recorded in Luke 10. It is good for clergy to be involved in
this, but ministrants do not have to be ordained, any more
than they need to have special individual gifts of healing:
'... those who *believe*... will place their hands on sick
people...', said Jesus before his ascension (Mark 16:17,18,
emphasis added), and so it is sufficient that those who minister are believers. This belief should be threefold. They
should believe in Jesus himself, in the reality and historicity
of his healing ministry, and in the validity of its continuation
through his body, the church, today. Personally, I think it
best if this ministry is not excessively individualised or
lengthy, because that distorts the shape of the service.
Additional ministry can be offered afterwards, but while the
service is under way I believe it is perfectly adequate for

ministrants to say a short prayer in unison, so that the two voices speaking together signify that their action represents the body of Christ giving the touch of Christ. I also believe that the focus of this prayer should be on God the Father, God the Son or God the Holy Spirit. As they lay their hands on the heads or shoulders of those who have come for ministry, they could, for instance, pray: 'God the Father hold you safe within his healing love'; or 'Jesus meet you at your deepest point of need'; or 'The healing life and power of the Holy Spirit be in you. Amen.'

An alternative is to use the moment when the Peace is passed around the congregation as the occasion for the body of Christ to give and receive the touch of Christ. If this happens, all who wish to do so find themselves becoming both recipients and ministrants, though it must be made possible for any who for some reason choose not to be part of the laying on of hands just to kneel and pray quietly. For those who do wish to participate (and in my experience most are happy to do so, after a careful explanation), the procedure can be a very simple one. On this occasion the Peace will not involve moving around, greeting each other, and exchanging hugs and handshakes (which may come as a relief to some!). Rather, each person will link hands with those on either side. Led from the front of the church, all will say in unison, phrase by phrase, a prayer that makes clear the Trinitarian resources that are undergirding the whole service. They will have been told in advance the wording of the prayer to be used, so that nobody is taken by surprise when it is said.

When I am conducting a healing Eucharist and it has been decided to use this method for the laying on of hands, I find that the Trinitarian prayer that comes to me, and which I lead clause by clause for the congregation to say as they hold and are held by one another, tends to be something like this:

God, Creator, Father,
re-create you, re-create me,
in body, mind and spirit.
Jesus, meet us
at our every point of need.
And the healing power of the Holy Spirit
be in you, be in me,
in time and for eternity.
Alleluia. Amen.

Thus the Peace becomes part of the every-member prayer ministry that should characterise each local church, and it can be no small revelation when it is demonstrated that real power can flow through ordinary believers in this way. I shall always remember the amazement on the face of a woman who had just laid hands on the man next to her, who had difficulty in walking, only to find that afterwards he put aside his stick and ran up and down a nearby flight of stairs.

There will be more in the next chapter about the power that this ministry can sometimes generate. But for the moment it is important to re-emphasise that the basis of Christian healing is simply the practice of the presence of Christ, and that our belief in this presence stems from the fundamental Christian conviction that, from the moment Jesus was liberated by the miracle of the ascension to range at will throughout time and space, his followers everywhere can take it as an article of faith that to worship in his name is actually to meet him, and to seek to live as a Christian is to learn to journey through life as those who walk in the company of the healing Christ, the King who is among us.

Chapter 11
The empowerment of Christian living

It has always seemed to me that one of the most difficult sayings in the whole of the New Testament comes in John 14:12. This records a double promise from Jesus. The first half is, in all conscience, hard enough to accept. Here our Lord says that 'anyone who has faith in me will do what I have been doing'. But whatever are we to make of the second half? For Jesus not only repeats this promise but actually 'upgrades' it! Believers, he says, will 'do even greater things than these'.

Now bear in mind that Jesus is reported to have fed 5,000 people with a handful of loaves and fishes, to have defied gravity by walking on water, to have changed the weather and stilled a storm, to have healed countless sick and diseased people, and even on occasion to have raised the dead. How can we possibly believe that people like you and me could not only be empowered to do something similar but might actually accomplish *greater* things?

One's first reaction is that thoughts like these must be concepts of cloud cuckoo land! What could possibly be the rational basis of a belief that any such thing could be remotely feasible? As I write about this text from John's

Gospel, I feel totally out of my depth. My guess is that you feel equally so as you read about it.

I suppose that in the past I have tended to classify this as a 'hard saying' and to file it away in the back of my mind under the heading, 'Things I must ask Jesus about in heaven'. But recently it has begun to strike me that, as so often happens, hitherto I have not been looking at the whole of the text.

In the full text, Jesus, because I guess he knows just how hard we shall find it to take in what he is about to say, starts with the words, 'I tell you the truth'. Then he continues: 'anyone who has faith in me will do what I have been doing. He will do even greater things than these' – and then he adds, 'because I am going to the Father'. In other words, this is a promise that, like so much in the New Testament, is fundamentally connected to the ascension. It was on the Mount of Ascension that Jesus promised his disciples, 'you will receive power ...' (Acts 1:8), and it is only as we stand with him there that we can put the words from John's Gospel in their proper context.

During the earthly ministry of Jesus his miracles were limited by the spatio-temporal restrictions he took upon himself at his incarnation. But when these spatio-temporal restrictions were removed at his ascension, it became possible for a new era to begin, in which the power of the kingdom of God could invade our world on a greater and wider scale. For from then on, wherever believers were to be found, there would Jesus be. As Martin Luther was subsequently to put it, each Christian is called to be a 'Christ' to his neighbour.[1]

At the risk of seeming to put my sanity in doubt, I want in the later part of this chapter to tell a series of what may be termed 'power stories', all based upon the practice of the presence of the ascended Christ and the consequential activity of the Holy Spirit. So there are going to be some heady moments as this chapter moves towards its end. But before that, three important disclaimers must be made.

First, for all involved in 'power ministry' it is better to under-promise and over-perform than vice versa. In fact, I wonder whether we should use that term at all. When, not long ago, a colleague talked to me about his personal 'power ministry', I could not help cringing. Surely it is better for any such talk to come from recipients than from ministrants. Only a recipient is truly qualified to say how powerful or not any individual act of ministry may have been.

Secondly, at the heart of both Scripture and experience there is a paradox. I have often been surprised to be told that it is precisely when I have felt lowest and weakest that my own ministry has been at its strongest. Paul says that this was his experience too. He wrote, '... when I am weak, then I am strong' (2 Cor 12:10).

Recently I have come to know an Indian clergyman, Dr Chris Gnanakan. He is currently in England at Leeds University, where he is writing a thesis on the subject of a remarkable healing evangelist, Dr Doraiswamy Geoffrey Samuel Dhinakaran, who is famous in India, although little known in the rest of the world. Chris Gnanakan tells me that Dr Dhinakaran is a classical example of weakness and power going hand in hand. As a child he suffered from polio. He has undergone two heart transplant operations and one kidney transplant. He is never a well man and is in constant need of medication. And yet he exercises a quite extraordinary preaching ministry, regularly attracting crowds of three hundred thousand people, and has been involved in many healing miracles, some of them witnessed and attested by Chris Gnanakan. Dr Dhinakaran has no doubt about the source of the power that flows through him in spite of his own weakness. It all rests on the practice of the presence of Christ, and was initiated by a mysterious three-hour face-to-face encounter with Jesus on 10 October 1962, which changed his life and then, through him, the lives of many more.

Thirdly, along with the paradox of 'strength through weakness' comes a host of problems and enigmas, which characterise any honest ministry of Christian healing. Channelling the power of God is certainly not a matter of taking up a magic wand that can make all difficulties disappear. On the contrary, Christian healing and Christian anguish seem to go hand in hand. I believe we should be deeply suspicious of any who seem to have no problems in their ministry and who tell only stories of success. Speaking personally, while writing this and the last chapter I have been suffering from a health problem I have found very difficult to bear. Say a prayer for me, if you will.

Having made these disclaimers, however, I find I cannot deny that ministry based on the practice of the presence of the ascended Christ, the King who is among us, sometimes generates an amazing and (in human terms) an inexplicable power. I believe that here and now in our own day we can find parallels to any of the extraordinary elements in the life of Jesus, which were listed at the beginning of this chapter. To select one at random, the feeding of the 5,000 may seem a million miles away from our own life in the twenty-first century, and yet the director of a Roman Catholic community not far from my home in Merseyside assures me that something similar happened in his own experience, at a time when a thousand unexpected hungry guests turned up at a conference.

The conference leaders decided that they must trust our Lord to deal with this situation, and so they started to serve their guests out of the provisions they had prepared, which consisted of a very limited amount of stew and bread sticks. Soon they were down to the bottom of the stew pot, but they continued to scrape away at the final portions and unaccountably there seemed to be something left until everybody had been fed. They had twenty bread sticks available, a quantity which could normally have served no more than eighty. Once again, as these were broken up and handed out, there always seemed to be more. When all had been fed, the remaining bread sticks were counted. There were still twenty! Inexplicably, the food seemed just to multiply for as long as it was necessary. I am aware that, humanly speaking, this is totally impossible, and yet the man who tells this story (and I phoned him before writing these words, in order to check the details once again) is someone whose word I would not normally dream of disbelieving.

As far as my own experience goes, accounts of the inexplicable power of God are most likely to be set within the context of the ministry of Christian healing, because that has been a major concern of mine for many years. Many such stories are recorded in my earlier books – especially in *The Practice of Christian Healing*,[2] *Finding Hope and Healing through the Bible*[3] and *How to Pray when Life Hurts*.[4] Here, for your consideration, is a selection of these stories (using fictional names). Some have been told before. Others are in print now for the first time.

First, let me tell a story alluded to briefly on page 24 of *The Practice of Christian Healing* and told more fully on pages 39,40 of *Finding Hope and Healing through the Bible*. It is a remarkable parallel to the story told in Mark 1:29–31, where Jesus healed Peter's mother-in-law of the fever that had confined her to her bed. In fact, it is in some ways even more remarkable.

When I became vicar of the parish of Prenton on the out-
skirts of Birkenhead, I felt it important that the ministry of
Christian healing should become an integral part of the life
of the two churches there. In order that this might be so, I
knew it was essential to have the support of the churchwar-
dens. One of them was a local dentist, Jim – a lovely, gentle
man, greatly respected in the local community. Soon after I
arrived he became very ill and was rushed into hospital with
a life-threatening condition, double viral pneumonia. When
I went to see Jim in his ward, the indications of his raging
temperature were obvious and very alarming. He had
developed what is sometimes called a 'Gethsemane sweat'.
Great droplets of perspiration were visibly erupting from
his skin and running in rivulets down his face. I had never
seen anything quite like it before. I asked him if I might offer
him the ministry of Christian healing, and explained that,
though I had no power in myself to affect the situation,
together we could practise the presence of Christ and my
hands could be used to give the touch of our Lord. He
readily agreed to this and I laid hands on him in the name of
Jesus. Afterwards I needed a towel to dry myself.

A few minutes after we had finished this act of prayer
ministry, a young nurse came to the bed with a thermometer. She explained that she had been instructed to record
his temperature every hour. After doing so, she told me that
the thermometer must be broken.

'According to this,' she said, 'his temperature is normal,
and that's not possible.'

She was back almost immediately with a second thermometer. She took Jim's temperature again – and then she
turned quite white. 'This is impossible,' she told me. 'It says
his temperature is absolutely normal, and it can't be so.'

But it was. Rather weakly, I said that perhaps he had

sweated it out of himself and took my leave.

Both Jim and I, however, knew what had happened. He went on to make a sound and steady recovery and, when he was back home again, he insisted on telling the whole story to our congregation in church. So it was that healing services began at both St Stephen's and St Alban's, Prenton, with the full support of the church leaders.

It is not often that one has immediate medical confirmation of the healing power of Christ, as happened with Jim. But that was also the case with Robert. Robert is a physiotherapist. He had to go into hospital for an operation on a major pelvic abscess, and, when he did so, he took with him a tape of some Christian music and an article I had written on the healing power that can be generated by practising the presence of Christ. The evening before the operation was due to take place, he read the article, turned on the tape and went off to sleep, claiming the presence of Jesus. Next morning it was discovered that the abscess had completely disappeared. This totally defied medical expectation. Robert subsequently sent me photocopies of the hospital documents dealing with his case, which he had been allowed to take home with him, including one written in the surgeon's own handwriting, confirming that inexplicably there was now 'no erythema, no swelling, no rectal horseshoe abscess, no pelvic abscess'. Robert wrote to me, 'I was and still am amazed and filled with wonder.'

It reminds me of a further instance of medically documented Christian healing, which I have not recorded in print till now. I heard it when I went to conduct a healing service at a church in Blackpool. When the service was over a young couple, Charles and Judith, came to me and said, 'We have absolutely no doubt that Jesus heals today, because we owe the life of our eldest child to him.' Little Victoria had been a microcephalic baby. Scans during the pregnancy revealed that right up to the thirty-sixth week, although Victoria's body grew, her head failed to do so. Judith was offered an abortion, but refused. After the final scan at the thirty-sixth week, Judith, Charles and the hospital staff set themselves to wait for the birth – with considerable apprehension.

What happened next was almost unbelievable. An unknown clergyman rang the front doorbell of the local vicarage and said that he had the strongest of convictions that he was meant to lay hands on somebody in that parish in the name of Jesus. After a moment of hesitation the vicar gave him the address of Charles and Judith and soon he was in their home. He explained that he felt called to give Judith the touch of Jesus and she accepted his offer.

During the last four weeks of Judith's pregnancy, Victoria's head grew to a normal size. This, I am assured, should have been impossible. After Victoria's birth, it seemed as though the whole hospital staff came to see Judith and her baby, and before they were discharged they were presented with photographs from the earlier scans, so that they would always have evidence of the medical miracle they had experienced. Charles and Judith often take these photos with them when they are invited to tell their story in other churches. As for Victoria, it was a real joy to see her playing at the back of that Blackpool church with her new little sister, both of them normal, healthy, lovely girls.

In the stories so far, the healing ministry has been in clerical or medical hands, but this is not how it necessarily has to be. An extraordinary sequence of events comes to mind, to which there is the briefest of references in *How to Pray when Life Hurts* (p 11). Perhaps this is the right time for me to record them in full, though I have to say that I do so with a degree of trepidation.

I had been invited to speak about the healing ministry in a suburban housegroup containing about twenty members. We enjoyed a pleasant evening together, during which I did my best to share the basic principles of Christian healing and to illustrate them with a few stories. Eventually the evening came to an end and I returned home, feeling that I had offered the group a reasonably decent presentation – and little guessing the bombshell that was shortly to go off.

Next day my phone rang. It was Philip, a young man who had been present at the housegroup. He was clearly excited.

'I want to thank you', he said, 'for all you said to us and gave to us last night. Since then I've been round to see my auntie. She has multiple sclerosis and is in a wheelchair. But I have told her all you said, and I've laid hands on her in the name of Jesus. I've promised her that soon her MS will have gone and that she'll be riding her bicycle again.' He went on, 'You know, I would never have done it without you. You have a wonderful faith. I'm so grateful for all you taught me. And so will Auntie be when she is healed!'

I was appalled. My mind was reeling. 'What have I done?' I thought. For one of the worst things you can do in the healing ministry is to give someone totally false hope, and it seemed to me that I had done just that. Immediately my mind went into overdrive and I started to plan a damage-limitation exercise.

'I'm so glad you found the evening such an interesting one,' I said as calmly as I could. 'You and I must keep in touch. I'll ring you again to see how things are going.'

A fortnight later I did so. 'How are you?' I asked him.

'Oh, I'm fine,' he said, 'and so is Auntie. She's out of her wheelchair now and is riding her bicycle again. There's no sign of MS any more!'

It was as well that he could not see my jaw drop.

Six months later I checked up again. Auntie was still up
and about and on her bike, and once again he made his original speech to me.

'I would never have done it without you,' he said. 'I wish
I had your faith!'

In some ways this is a story without a moral. It breaks all
the rules of good practice that I have come to work out over
the years, and I am certainly not suggesting that any reader
should attempt anything like it. Over the years, however, I
have had to accept that God is not necessarily bound by
rules of good practice. Clearly, he warmed to Auntie in her
need and to Philip with his simple, uncomplicated, adven-
turous faith. It would seem that you never know what may
happen when a young Christian claims the presence and the
healing power of the ascended Christ.

Other stories of healing flood into my mind as I write this
chapter. There was Madeleine, a teacher whose vocal chords
had been damaged during the course of a throat operation.
Her voice returned to her in full strength during a healing
service in one of our cathedrals. I remember hearing and
seeing the excitement around her as it happened. Once
again I checked twice during the months that followed to
make sure that this was a lasting development for her. Then
there was Edwina, whose hearing returned to her during a
school of healing prayer I conducted in the Isle of Man.
There was Annie, who could hardly walk before she
attended one of our healing services, but afterwards could
not only walk but also run. There was Norah, who told me
she had the strongest feeling that her cancer was being dealt
with during one of these services. She was right. The cancer
left her and did not return till many years later, just before
she died. Then there was Sally, who attended our healing
services not for herself but to pray for her husband, who had

been diagnosed as suffering from cancer. Month by month she reported to us that the cancer was shrinking. Gradually it reduced from the size of an orange to that of a pea, before it finally disappeared. Her husband, who was not a believer, was amazed at what was happening. 'I don't know what you're doing at that church of yours,' he said, 'but whatever it is, keep it up, girl!'

Before this sequence of stories comes to an end, perhaps I may be allowed to tell just one more, because it happened fairly recently in my own home and is still fresh in my mind. Nigel, a retired minister, turned up on our front doorstep to ask for prayer because he had lost nearly all the movement in his neck, and feared that if it became totally rigid he would no longer be able to drive his car. My wife and I did as he asked and then before our eyes his neck slowly began to move. His head turned first to the left and then to the right, then further to the left and further to the right. It continued to do this until he had recovered virtually normal neck movement. My wife Eira, a chartered physiotherapist, said she had never seen anything like it in all her medical experience. I should stress that we were not manipulating him in any way, but were just holding him by our prayers within the presence of the ascended Christ.

Accounts of healings such as these could continue for many more pages. There are scores more that I could extract and amplify from earlier books, and scores too that have not yet been told. But to make sure that we all remain firmly rooted in reality, I suggest that it may be right at this time to read once again the three disclaimers to be found earlier in this chapter. It is also important to say that, for reasons I do not understand, often the way in which God's power is shown is *not* by a miraculous change in circumstances but by an infusion of remarkable inner strength into either sufferers or carers or both. I think for instance of a colleague in the ministry who has willingly taken total responsibility for his disabled wife. She cannot speak and can hardly move. Her life is spent either in bed or in a wheelchair. I often pray for her healing, but there is no sign that it is going to happen. What has happened, however, is that her husband has discovered an enormous inner strength and grace. Against all the odds he radiates happiness. Recently he actually said to me, 'Roy, you have no idea what a privilege it is to have the total responsibility for someone whom you love entirely in your hands.' He is right. I have absolutely no idea how he can feel this way. All that I and others can do is to watch and to marvel. For here too is a notable illustration of empowerment for Christian life. In some ways it seems more of a miracle than any of the others.

I have selected the stories in this chapter carefully – and have in fact deliberately omitted some of the most mystifying ones, in case I should lose credibility. But if you should want to read of things that are *really* strange, you can find them in some of my earlier writings. For instance, you could turn up the account of a Church Army captain who apparently died but was prayed back to life while he lay on the slab in the hospital mortuary. It was told in one of my first books, *Invitation to Healing*[5] (p 93–97). In my more recent book, *The Practice of Christian Healing* [6] (p 111,112), you can read how, in order that I could minister to a young girl whose life was in danger, it seems I was either set in some sort of time warp or was otherwise enabled to be in two places at the same time!

I am aware that to suggest that death and time and space may occasionally loosen their grasp upon us may seem to take us into realms of pure science fiction. And yet perhaps not. Maybe we should not judge it incredible if, when we claim the promise of our ascended King to be among us, we find that from his para-cosmic perspective he is able to operate on the very edge of death, both within and beyond our understanding of time and space. All of which brings us to our final chapter and to the most mysterious subject of all.

Chapter 12
The gate of heaven

In the sitting-room of our home on the Wirral coast, Eira and I have the pleasure of looking out through a large picture window straight on to the Irish Sea. Day by day, we can see container ships and ferries and occasional passenger liners setting out from the port of Liverpool, steaming to the distant horizon, and there disappearing from our sight.

We know of course that when these ships pass from our view they do not cease to exist. They voyage on to destinations that are beyond our sight but none the less real for that. The limits of our perception are just that – limits of 'perception'. They do not represent the absolute nature of things. I was taught this fact at school, though it did not become a personal reality for me until I first went up in an aeroplane and actually saw the horizon expand before my eyes.

Jesus teaches that what is true of space is also true of time. In terms of time, our horizon – the point beyond which we cannot see – is death. In our life on earth one moment is followed by another, one day by another, one year by another, until our moments and days and years on earth come to an end. At this point time appears to run out and we appear to terminate. This is our perception. But it is only a perception,

and if Jesus is to be believed it is not a correct one. He went
to some trouble to teach his followers that horizons in time
are no more absolute than horizons in space, and that we
were created not just to experience time on earth but also to
explore the mystery of eternity.

Initially, the disciples seemed to have had some difficulty
with the concept of eternal life. They trusted Christ's teaching but, before they could see beyond the horizon of time in
any personal way, they needed an experience rather like my
aeroplane trip. This happened to them at the ascension.
Jesus knew that this would be so and he prepared his followers for it. He told his disciples: '... he who believes has
everlasting life. I am the bread of life' (John 6:47,48). He said,
'... he who feeds on this bread will live for ever' (John 6:58).
We are told that his hearers were perplexed at this statement:
'On hearing it, many of his disciples said, "This is a hard
teaching. Who can accept it?"' (John 6:60). Jesus' answer
was, 'Does this offend you? What if you see the Son of Man
ascend to where he was before!' (John 6:61,62).

In this final chapter, our aim will be to consider the
mystery of eternal life. As we do so our vantage point will
be upon that mountain where the disciples saw the Son of
Man 'ascend to where he was before'. We shall seek to
benefit from the unique perspective that can come to us
there – and only there. For it is at the ascension that time and
eternity uniquely intersect.

First, however, we must put in place some of the initial
building blocks that have led humankind to construct the-
ories about the possibility of life after death. For this belief,
though it flies in the face of all the physical evidence, has
cropped up with an awkward persistence since the earliest
days of the human race. One of the facts known about Stone
Age man is that he buried his dead, often with valuable tools,

weapons and cooking utensils. Stone was used for sepul-
chres long before it was used to house the living. As the centuries went by, humankind did not discard whatever
instincts had made our ancestors do these things. On the contrary, the feeling that there may be life after death has been
retained and embellished from generation to generation.

Many of the factors that have led to this have nothing to
do with either the Christian faith or any of the other major
world religions. They seem to be rooted in our experience of
the mystery of life and our own interior sense of being. They
have emerged both through philosophical debate and
through mystical visions. And this ongoing process of
thought and revelation has been augmented and reinforced
by a host of inexplicable phenomena, ranging from apparent encounters with 'ghosts' and other paranormal pres-
ences to strange out-of-the-body experiences, which, it
seems, can occur at any point in life, but particularly at the
edge of death. I have written about these factors elsewhere
(see *Christ With Us*,[1] Chapter 10), and will not repeat the
details here. Though none of these considerations is specifically Christian, this certainly does not mean that
Christianity has no contribution to make in this area.
Speaking personally, my own main reasons for believing
that death is not meant to be the end of us are almost all
bound up with the Christian faith, and especially with the
doctrine of the Holy Trinity.

If I believe in God the Father, then it is hard to avoid some
sort of concept of life after death. For if a Father-God exists,
who is both almighty and all-loving, then it seems to follow,
not just as a matter of faith but of logic, that nothing he
deems to be of value within his creation can ever be wasted.
He has certainly shown us, both by the infinite trouble he
took over our creation and by all that he has done for us

through his Son Jesus, that he regards us to be of value. So it really would seem that he has more in mind for us than an insignificant and transitory place on the scrap heap of time.

Then, too, if we believe that Jesus is God the Son, we can hardly suppose that death has ultimate power over us. There are three reasons for this.

One lies in his unambiguous teaching on this subject. Jesus speaks plainly about eternal life in all four Gospels. For example, Matthew records Christ's injunction to 'store up for yourself treasures in heaven ...' (Matt 6:20). Mark records the promise that those who make sacrifices for the sake of Christ will receive 'in the age to come, eternal life' (Mark 10:30). Luke tells us that the children of the resurrection 'can no longer die; for they are like the angels ...' (Luke 20:36). And John preserves for us the precious promise that 'God so loved the world that he gave his one and only Son, that whoever believes in him shall not perish but have eternal life' (John 3:16).

The second reason is that Jesus not only spoke about eternal life. He actually demonstrated it by his own resurrection from the dead. In *Christ With Us* I have listed the many considerations that convince me that his resurrection is no fable but a solid historical fact, massively attested by a wealth of evidence.

As we shall see as this chapter continues, the third factor in the life of Christ that points unambiguously to life after death is the ascension.

Furthermore, if faith in the Father and the Son leads to belief in life after death, so too does the doctrine of God the Holy Spirit. For if the Holy Spirit is divine and if we are called to receive him and become one with him, it would seem logically inescapable that those who are irradiated by his essence must have something of eternity in them.

Many other world religions teach life after death for reasons of their own. We need not go into them here, but it is not surprising that when all the factors, both religious and non-religious, are added together, the case for accepting some kind of survival beyond death has seemed so strong to so many. Professor C D Broad, former Knightsbridge Professor of Moral Philosophy at Cambridge, made no secret of the fact that personally he had no desire for life after death, yet he came to the reluctant conclusion that the evidence for it is stronger than the evidence against it.[2]

There is, then, considerable agreement about the possibility that there may well be life after death; and there is no shortage of books arguing this case. It is a different matter, however, if we ask not whether it exists but '... what will it be like?'

Here there is more reticence and a great deal less consensus. If we can achieve an ascension perspective, however, we shall have unique advantages in seeking an answer. For at the ascension Jesus not only drew back the veil on life after death as a general concept, but did so in a way that was of high personal relevance to you and to me. He had promised this earlier. 'I am going,' he told his disciples, and us too if we seek to follow him. '... I am going ... to prepare a place for you' (John 14:2).

What do we learn as we try to stand on the Mount of Ascension with his disciples and to consider this promise? We certainly learn that the most popular notions of life after death are very wide of the biblical mark. My guess is that if we were to ask a cross section of the general public how they picture the nature of survival after death, most would say that, once our soul leaves our present body, from then on existence will in no way be a physical experience. We will be ethereal, insubstantial, non-solid.

The Bible, however, says no such thing. In fact, it says precisely the opposite. Far from having no body, we will find ourselves equipped with a 'super-body'. If our trust is in Jesus, then ultimately 'we shall be like him' (1 John 3:2). The risen and ascended Christ is not only our forerunner as he conquers death and returns to heaven; he is also the prototype of all we are destined to become. If we want to learn about eternal life, we must study the accounts of his resurrection appearances up to and including the moment of his ascension, as they are recorded in the Gospels and at the beginning of Acts. As we do so, we rapidly see that after death Jesus was very far from being a spectre or wraith. He was gloriously physical. His new body was substantial and tangible. Thomas was able to touch him and feel him (John 20:27). It is true that in order to encounter Thomas, Jesus passed through a locked door (John 20:26), but, if I read Scripture correctly, this was not because he was now less solid than the door, it was because he was now actually *more* solid than the door. It was rather like the way I can walk through mist and smoke, because I am more solid than they are.

Maybe this idea is not all that surprising. A friend who teaches physics at Liverpool University tells me that life on this earth is nothing like as solid as we usually take it to be. The desk at which I sit to write these words is actually mostly composed of space! So am I. So are you. Perhaps, as a former classicist, I should be prepared for this thought. For my mind goes back to Plato's *Republic* with its suggestion that life here and now is rather like a series of shadows cast by a more real world, which presently is just out of our sight.

In any event, according to Scripture the risen Jesus was not sub-physical. He was 'supra-physical'. This was his nature as he ascended into heaven, and this is the nature of the eternal life that he offers us. The Bible could hardly make it plainer. 'He will change our weak mortal bodies and make them like his own glorious body, using that power by which he is able to bring all things under his rule' (Phil 3:21, Good News Bible).

Back in Chapter 2 of this book we asked the question, 'Where did Jesus go at the ascension and where is he now in these post-ascension days?' The answer I suggested is that he went to, and is now in, what I termed a 'larger place', more solid, more substantial, more real than the world we now inhabit. If this is true, it follows that, when we go to the place he has prepared for us, we too shall need to be more solid, more substantial, more real.

It is a revealing and exciting exercise to study chapters in Scripture such as 1 Corinthians 15 and 2 Corinthians 5, in which Paul compares the limitations of our present bodies with the freedom, the power and the shining glory of that which is to be. He has no doubt that life in our forthcoming 'spiritual body', as he likes to call it, will represent a considerable advance on our present physical experience. He says it will be like living in a permanent building, rather than in a fragile tent as we do at this moment (2 Cor 5:1). The new body, says Paul, will be beautiful and strong, no matter how ugly and weak our mortal body may have become in the final days of this life (1 Cor 15:43).

But a further question leaps to our mind as we think about this. If, by the grace of God, you and I are to receive new, exciting super-bodies, just what is it that we shall be called to do with them, when we keep company with our ascended Lord in the kingdom of heaven? If by any chance you have a mental picture of putting on a nightshirt, sitting on a damp cloud and doing nothing for all eternity except perhaps having an occasional pluck at a harp, do get rid of it. This is a misconception that, for all its popularity, is supported neither by Scripture nor by common sense. There is no way we could stand anything like that as a way of life for ever and ever.

The biblical picture of eternal life is totally different. Although the writers of Scripture know that, while we are within a time sequence, the concept of eternity must be well beyond our powers of imagination, for all that they have some tantalising hints and clues to offer us. Even though eternal truth must defy earthly description, the picture they offer is remarkably homely. Perhaps this is because so much of it is derived from Jesus himself, and he was a past master at expressing the inexpressible in familiar language and simple parables.

The Bible invites us to picture a shining city within a cosmopolitan kingdom. It is full of purposeful activity and its citizens enjoy life to the full. Wrong relationships are a thing of the past. People there feel right with God, right with each other and right with all creation. Exciting new dimensions of worship have a central and natural place in their lives. Also – and this may be a surprise – they regularly go to great parties. In fact, heaven is sometimes described as the wedding reception to end all wedding receptions. There is superb food, fine wine and marvellous company. Everyone celebrates the close, new relationship that all have with the Son of God, a relationship as close and good as that of the best marriage you can imagine on earth. Heaven is described as a place of light, of love and of continual discovery. Nobody is bored, because eternal life is quite simply the best there could be. Imagine whatever is most precious to you in this life. Heaven will be better than that. And though it will be the absolute and incomparable best, yet paradoxically it will keep getting better and better, because the new body, the new mind and the new spirit of each citizen will experience eternal growth and development and the adventure of exploring God's own infinity.

Let me lay a trail of scriptural texts to show the basis of this picture of heaven. Look them up if you wish.

> *Matthew 8:11* The cosmopolitan kingdom
>
> *Matthew 22:4* Partying and feasting at a great wedding reception
>
> *Matthew 26:29* The next time you receive Holy Communion, remember Jesus described it as a fore-taste of the wine of the kingdom of heaven
>
> *Revelation 19:1–8* The new dimensions of worship
>
> *Luke 10:25–28* The loving relationships at the heart of life in the heavenly city
>
> *Matthew 13:44,45* The picture of eternal life as the very best that there could possibly be; the parables of the hidden treasure and the pearl of great price
>
> *Matthew 13:31* The growth principle within the kingdom of heaven
>
> *1 Corinthians 2:9* An acknowledgement that all of this is a mystery that is beyond us for the moment
>
> *1 John 3:2* The central conviction that at the heart of the mystery there is Jesus himself

Some Christians have asked when all of this will come into being, and it has to be admitted that there is a degree of ambiguity about the answer given by Scripture. In 1 Thessalonians 4:13–18 a future day of resurrection is spoken of, whereas Luke 23:43 seems to imply that eternal life can begin at the moment of physical death. Perhaps both are true, the first from the standpoint of this world, the second from the perspective of an eternity that is beyond time.

As far as the early followers of Jesus were concerned, from the very moment that Jesus ascended into heaven they could never be sure just when the veil of heaven might be temporarily lifted for any one of them. Thus we are told that, before Stephen died, he 'looked up to heaven and saw the glory of God, and Jesus standing at the right hand of God' (Acts 7:55). Similarly, Paul tells us that he knows 'a man' who was 'caught up to the third heaven' and 'heard inexpressible things, things that man is not permitted to tell' (2 Cor 12:2–4). It is usually assumed that this 'man' he knows is none other than Paul himself. John is another who tells us that he too was enabled to see 'a door standing open in heaven' (Rev 4:1).

Christians are sometimes similarly privileged today. In my own family, my grandfather on my mother's side, after recovering from a severe illness, told me confidentially that he had been allowed a glimpse of heaven. He was a professional musician and his principal memory of this experience was that the music of heaven was truly awesome. On my father's side of the family, my grandmother also claimed a glimpse of heaven before she died. Her husband and her sons and daughters were standing around her bed as she lay dying, and she told them of the unspeakable beauty that she was seeing through the veil between time and eternity and that, though she loved them all, she now found herself desiring to move on more than anything else.

Who knows whether you and I may at some point be granted a similar foretaste? If we are not, we must just wait for our time to come. In the meantime, while we are waiting, our life should certainly not be characterised by that fear of death and the unknown that is the mark of so many, but rather by a sort of homesickness for the place Jesus has prepared for us. Paul tells us of his own homesickness for heaven and for the yearning he experienced for the kingdom of the ascended Christ. He suggests that his readers should feel the same way: '... set your hearts on things above, where Christ is seated at the right hand of God. Set your minds on things above, not on earthly things' (Col 3:1,2).

This yearning can only be enhanced by the rhapsodic writing of John, as he stretches human language to its limits, in his description of the heavenly city:

I saw a new heaven and a new earth. The first heaven and the first earth disappeared, and the sea vanished. And I saw the Holy City, the new Jerusalem, coming down out of heaven from God, prepared and ready, like a bride dressed to meet her husband. I heard a loud voice speaking from the throne: 'Now God's home is with mankind! He will live with them, and they shall be his people. God himself will be with them, and he will be their God. He will wipe away all tears from their eyes. There will be no more death, no more grief or crying or pain. The old things have disappeared.'

Then the one who sits on the throne said, 'And now I make all things new!'

Revelation 21:1–5, Good News Bible

How can one possibly follow words like these? Certainly not by asking *where* this holy city might be located. In the context of eternity that question would have no more meaning than asking when it will come into being. For, as we have already seen, eternity cannot be confined within dimensions of time and space. It is greater, larger, more real than our little minds can yet conceive, limited as we still are by the boundaries of our own space-time continuum.

There is, however, one further question we can (and indeed must) ask. It is this. How can you and I be sure that we personally will find a place within the newborn community of the celestial city? Can we presume to believe not just in eternal life as a general concept but in our *own* eternal life?

It is vital to raise this issue because Jesus makes it clear that we humans have no automatic entitlement to a place in the kingdom of heaven. Indeed, the very opposite is true. Though we were created in the image of God (Gen 1:26), we have allowed that image to become blurred and distorted. We are a damaged species and are stupidly prone to resist all God's attempts to heal us. The sins that we commit, spawned by the dark side of our own nature, can and do separate us from God, from one another and from God's will that we should enjoy eternal life with him. In fact, our destination would be what Jesus calls 'outer darkness' (Matt 22:13, Authorised Version), where self-torment leads ultimately to self-destruction, were it not for the extraordinary opportunity that God generously gives us and that is the heart of the Christian gospel.

Paul says that 'sin pays its wage – death; but God's free gift is eternal life in union with Christ Jesus our Lord' (Rom 6:23, Good News Bible). Our place in heaven depends on our relationship with Jesus. It was for our sake that he came into this world. It was for us that he died upon the cross. He rose from the dead for our sake. And now this same Jesus, our ascended King, holds the gates of heaven open for us, if we accept him as our Saviour, Lord and Friend. Jesus can do for us that which we are totally incapable of doing for ourselves. This is the heart and essence of the Christian gospel.

How else, then, could I end this enquiry into the meaning of the ascension of Christ than by offering you a prayer, which, if you wish, you can make your own. As I write it, I am going to say it for myself, and I invite you to join with me. I believe that God can and will use it to bring us nearer to himself and to prepare us for our journey into eternal life. 'He who has the Son', says John, 'has life ...' (1 John 5:12). Because of his ascension he is available now.

And so...

Jesus, I know that I am a sinner, and I am truly sorry for the wrongs I have done, but I also know that you love me and gave yourself for me. You rose from the dead and ascended into heaven. You are available to me here and now. You are the King who is among us and you offer to be at my side and in my life.

Gratefully I accept your offer to be my Saviour, my Lord and my Friend. Gratefully I accept your offer of forgiveness and a place in your kingdom.

I put my trust in you and want you at work in me, healing me, leading me, living in me. Ascended King, I ask for your help and strength that I may use my life in your service.

Thank you for all you are going to do in me, both here and in eternity. Amen.

References

Chapter 1: The forgotten festival

1   Sermones 53.4, *Collectio Selecta SS Ecclesiae Patrum*, ed D
    A B Caillau, p vii.

2   *Commentary on Acts*, on Acts 1:9.

3   *Ep ad Januarium* LIV, i.

Chapter 2: What happened on the mountain?

1   Geoffrey Bles, 1946.

2   *The Great Divorce*, p 112.

Chapter 4: A festival of kingship

1   See Michael Green, *Evangelism in the Early Church*,
    Hodder & Stoughton, 1970, p 210

2   PO Box 99, New Malden, Surrey KT3 3YF. Tel. 020 8942
    8810. Email: CSW@csw.org.uk

3   PO Box 54, Orpington, Kent BR5 9RT. Tel. 01689 823491.
    Email: info@releaseinternational.org

4   St John's, Cranleith Road, Wonersh, Guildford, Surrey
    GU5 OQX. Tel. 01483 894787.
    Email: info@jubileeaction.co.uk

Chapter 6: The festival of the Christ who is with us

1   SPCK, 2000.

2 Marshall, Morgan & Scott, 1977.

3 Pan, 1996.

Chapter 7: A bridge to Pentecost

1 SPCK, 2002, p 47, article 'Charismatic Renewal'.

2 *How to Pray when Life Hurts*, SU, 2003².

Chapter 8: A promise of the final coming

1 C S Lewis, *The Problem of Pain*, Geoffrey Bles, 1940, p 6.

2 Magnet, 1978, p 136.

Chapter 9: The heart of prayer

1 SU, 2003².

Chapter 10: The basis of Christian healing

1 Church House Publishing, 2000.

Chapter 11: The empowerment of Christian living

1 Martin Luther, *'Treatise on Christian Liberty'*, *Works of Martin Luther* (Philadelphia: Muhlenberg Press, 1947), p 337.

2 SPCK, 1998.

3 SPCK, 2000.

4 SU, 2003².

5 Kingsway, 1979.

6 SPCK, 1998.

Chapter 12: The gate of heaven

1 SU, 1997.

2 See Arnold Toynbee and others, *Man's Concern with Death*, Hodder & Stoughton, 1968, p 245,246.

Other Resources
from Scripture Union

How to Pray when Life Hurts
Roy Lawrence
ISBN 1 85999 674 4, £6.99
With wisdom and sensitivity born of wide experience, Roy Lawrence writes of the Christ who can bring healing and hope to the darkest situation. His book offers practical help for anyone facing hurt, guilt, pressure, anger, fear, or any of life's great traumas. This updated and expanded edition of a best-seller is also an excellent resource for those engaged in pastoral ministry.
B format, 144 pages

Make Me a Channel
Roy Lawrence
ISBN 1 85999 015 0, £4.99
The author highlights the struggle many Christians have in achieving a balance between receiving from God and giving to others. Written in a light-hearted style, the book also includes a guide for small group use.
B format, 160 pages

Oriel's Diary
Robert Harrison
ISBN 1 85999 684 1, £6.99
The personal diary of Archangel Oriel, colleague of Gabriel and Michael, records the birth, life, death and resurrection of Jesus Christ. Closely based on Luke's Gospel, *Oriel's Diary* presents an entirely original view of a familiar story. Author Robert Harrison describes his book as 'a mixture of biblical fact and creative fictionalisation'. His model is Jesus himself. 'Jesus deliberately communicated his message in stories because they hold divine truth more effectively than intellectual debate.' Engage your heart and imagination with this compelling, humorous and moving story.
Demy, 208 pages

Oriel's Travels

Robert Harrison

ISBN 1 85999 786 4, £6.99

From fanatical destroyer of the followers of Jesus to fearless gospel pioneer - the incredible story of the man central to the formation of the church!

Political wranglings at the highest level ... personal animosities at the lowest ... the mystery of how the church - 'the Boss's new family' - was birthed in the midst of fierce earthly discords and intense spiritual battles is described through the travel diary of Archangel Oriel. Oriel's mission appears simple - to make sure one man, Paul, gets to Rome, taking the good news about the resurrected Christ into the heart of the non-Jewish world. But Oriel's task is hindered by internal disagreements and external plots, forced flights and hair-raising escapes, ship-wreck and imprisonment ... not to mention his own deep fears of the sea and Paul's distrust of both horses and women!

Demy, 208 pages

Tracks across the Beach

Peter Smith

Illustrator: Graham Clarke

ISBN 185999 486 5, £9.99

In these meditations on glorious landscapes by the world-renowned illustrator Graham Clarke, Peter Smith relates each picture to both biblical passages and to moving stories of his experiences as a schoolteacher. His down-to-earth approach makes it easy for readers to apply the lessons he draws out of the passages to themselves.

255 x 210 mm 64 pages cased

Teamwork: How to Build Relationships

Gordon and Rosemary Jones

ISBN 1 85999 691 4, £7.99

This expanded and updated edition of a widely used book explores different aspects of teamwork. Designed as a readable and interesting workbook, it suggests ways in which people can work together harmoniously, especially in a mission context. It also has application, however, to many other areas: family life, university, the workplace and the local church.

Demy, 288 pages

90,000 Hours

Managing the World of Work

Rodney Green

ISBN 1 85999 594 2, £6.99

Most of us will spend 90,000 hours of our lives at work. How do we view this time? Does God want us to see our work as worthwhile in itself? Examining the themes of creativity, rest, harmony and perseverance from a biblical perspective, Rodney Green argues that this is indeed the case.

B format, 160 pages

It Makes Sense

A Handbook for Living

Stephen Gaukroger

ISBN 185999 743 0, £4.99

This revised edition of a best-seller offers humorous and compelling reasons why it makes sense to become a Christian. It has a proven track record as an evangelistic tool. Topics covered include science, suffering and other faiths. 'The best to shove into someone's hand the second they become a Christian.' Alpha

B format, 144 pages

Thank God it's Monday

Ministry in the Workplace

Mark Greene

ISBN 1 85999 208 0, £5.99

Fun, fast, and full of stories, this highly practical book looks at how we can make the most of the time we spend at work. This updated and expanded edition includes a new chapter on the ethical challenges that face us.

B format, 180 pages

Christian Life and Work package

(Video editor: Rob Purbrick)

ISBN 1 85999 532 2, £25.00

A six-part 2 hour video keyed into Mark Greene's book Thank God it's Monday. Includes a leader's guide and a copy of the book. Topics include, 'Introducing a Theology of Work', 'Evangelism in the Workplace', 'Relating to the Boss', 'Truthtelling and Handling Pressure at Work', and 'Work & Spirituality'. Presenters: Mark Greene and others.

A format pb 192 pages + workbook 60 pages + video

Christian Life and Today's World package

(Video editor: Rob Purbrick)
ISBN 1 85999 576 4, £25.00
How can we take up the challenge of living as Christians in a postmodern society? From SU and London Bible College comes another stimulating small group resource containing video, accompanying workbook for group leaders and book of articles written by members of the LBC faculty.
A format pb 192 pages + workbook 60 pages + video

Knowing God's Ways

A user's guide to the Old Testament
J Patton Taylor
ISBN 1 85999 349 4, £6.99
Do you find the Old Testament difficult to get into? If you've been looking for some help in making sense of it all, then this book by a professor at Union Theological College in Belfast is what you've been looking for! His accessible, user-friendly approach will help you gain a clear overview of the Old Testament, understand different genres, and apply biblical teaching to today's world.
Demy, 240 pages

Encounter with God: Every Day for a Year

Andrew Clark (ed)
ISBN 1 85999 670 1, £9.99
This handsome hardback contains a year's readings from key biblical books such as Exodus, John, Ephesians and Hebrews. In a selection form the best of the last four years' notes from *Encounter with God*, SU's in-depth Bible reading notes, well-known teachers explain and apply passages in a spiritually satisfying way.
210 x 148mm cased, 416 pages

The Lost Art of Meditation

Deepening your Prayer Life
Sheila Pritchard
ISBN 1 85999 643 4, £5.99
If you long to explore creative, two-way communication with the God of the universe and would love familiar Scriptures to seem fresh and new again... this book is for you. Discover the link between prayer and biblical meditation with popular *Closer to God* writer Sheila Pritchard. The book has many 'try it' suggestions.
B format, 128 pages

The Edge of Two Worlds

Exploring Christian Spirituality

Tony Kidd

ISBN: 1 85999 591 8, £4.99

Ever wondered about the place of confession, the Bible, silent contemplation, feelings and intercessions in Christian spirituality? Tony Kidd gives Bible passages, meditations and group discussions, questions to help us explore these areas. Endorsed by the Archbishop of York, this book is ideal for Lent courses but also suitable for other purposes.

B format, 80 pages

Dangerous Praying

Inspirational Ideas for individuals and groups

David Spriggs

ISBN: 1 85999335 4, £6.99

Drawing on Paul's letter to the Ephesians, this creative book challenges us to be bold when we pray, both in what we pray for and how we pray. David Spriggs presents us with 101 practical ideas and strategies to help us develop a courageous prayer life, whether in a group or individually.

B format, 160 pages

Ready to Grow

Practical steps to knowing God better

Alan Harkness

ISBN 0 949720 71 2, £5.99

An attractive and practical book written to encourage believers to make time with God a regular part of their lives. Includes chapters on preparation, getting started, the practicalities, sharing what you have learned, and different methods of combining Bible reading and prayer.

188mm x 125mm, 176 pages

Weak Enough for God to Use

Dennis Lennon

ISBN 1 85999 290 0, £4.99

This thoughtful, well-written book inspires us to believe that God uses ordinary people to do significant things for him. Character studies of Moses, David, Jeremiah and Mary combine with contemporary stories of people known to the author who have made an impact on the world around them.

A format, 160 pages

Faith and Common Sense

Living boldly, choosing wisely
David Dewey
ISBN 1 85999 302 8, £2.50 (bargain price)

This unusual book explores how we can live riskily yet sensibly. Drawing on the lives of key Bible characters like Peter, the author first lays a solid biblical and theological foundation for achieving a balance. Then follows a practical look at areas in our lives where a need for that balance is vital - healing, the gifts of the Spirit, work, money, failure and guidance.

A format, 128 pages

The Bible Unwrapped

Developing your Bible skills
David Dewey
ISBN 1 85999 533 0, £5.99

Is the Bible something of a closed book to you? Here you'll find help in finding your way around the Bible, and in grasping the big picture of the Bible's message. You'll also learn to appreciate the different types of literature in the Bible and be introduced to eight different approaches to Bible study. Clear and accurate charts and diagrams and a helpful glossary add value.

B Format, 160 pages

Understanding the Bible

John Stott
ISBN 1 85999 640 X, £5.99

A newly revised edition of a widely-acclaimed classic bestseller. Outstanding Christian teacher and author John Stott examines the cultural, social, geographical and historical background of the Bible, outlining the story and explaining the message. This new edition features focus questions at the beginning of each chapter, new up-to-date maps, and a full index.

B format pb, 214 pages

Understanding the Bible

John Stott
ISBN 1 85999 569 1, £9.99

A brand new edition in full colour. Revised and updated text is illustrated with charts, diagrams and wonderful colour photos. An ideal gift!

245x160mm hb, 170 pages

Small Group Resources

Connect Bible Studies

Over 15 titles available, £3.00/£3.50

Innovative, thought-provoking group Bible studies exploring key issues raised by contemporary films, TV programmes, books and music. Four weeks of material with a separate theme in each book. Prepared by Damaris Trust. A4, 48pp

LifeBuilder Bible Studies

Various authors

Each £3.50

Trustworthy and reliable, with 10 million sold worldwide, *LifeBuilders* are the market leader for small group Bible study. With over 80 titles to choose from, they cover all the New Testament and most key Old Testament books. As well as the studies on biblical books, there are others on biblical characters, and also a wide range of topical studies. Leader's notes are included. 210 x 140mm, most 64pp, some longer

The Re:action series

Kate Hayes

6 titles, each £3.50

These studies are for groups looking for material with quality discussion questions and strong links to everyday life. Thought-provoking material suitable for all ages, with no background knowledge needed. Ideal for post-Alpha groups. 210 x 140mm 48pp

Equipped for living

Florence MacKenzie

4 titles, each £3.50

A series designed for Christians wanting interactive Bible study in an engaging, style. Thought-provoking questions for personal reflection and application to life as well as group discussion. Between 8 and 10 studies in each book. 210 x 140mm 80pp

Visit church@home, SU's free online magazine for the world of small groups: www.scriptureunion.org.uk/churchathome

For other resources, access our web site (www.scriptureunion.org.uk) or ring 08450 706006 to request details of all our titles. Order from your Christian retailer or directly from SU.